Jewish Baltimore

Also by Gilbert Sandler

The Neighborhood: The Story of Baltimore's Little Italy

Baltimore Glimpses Revisited

GILBERT SANDLER

Jewish

THE JOHNS HOPKINS UNIVERSITY PRESS

Baltimore

A FAMILY ALBUM

BALTIMORE AND LONDON

IN ASSOCIATION WITH THE JEWISH MUSEUM OF MARYLAND

All images, unless otherwise credited, are courtesy
of the Jewish Museum of Maryland.

The Johns Hopkins University Press
2715 North Charles Street
Baltimore, Maryland 21218-4363
www.press.jhu.edu

Library of Congress cataloging-in-publication data will be
found at the end of this book.
A catalog record for this book is available from the British Library.

ISBN 0-8018-6427-5

This book is dedicated to the Jewish Museum of Maryland, to the Associated Jewish Community Federation of Baltimore, and to all who, in their service, helped create and nurture the remarkable Baltimore Jewish community.

And to my wife, Joan, for forbearance. To my children, for listening. And to my grandchildren—may they cherish the legacy!

Contents

The Way We Were

Epilogue: Owings Mills and Beyond, Still Moving North and West

Preface and Acknowledgments

Jewish Baltimore: A Family Album, it has to be said at the outset, is only part history. It is also journalism and memoir. Taken together, these thirty-six pieces are my attempt to capture, a thousand words at a time, the times, events, people, and moods of the Baltimore Jewish community from about the 1850s to 2000. For my sources, I have drawn generously from the archives of the Enoch Pratt Library, Maryland Historical Society, the *Baltimore Sun*, the Jewish Museum of Maryland, and interviews with people who were there, or who knew people who were. The task of what to include has been a daunting one. In the end, with the help of friends and colleagues, I strove for balance in facts, tone, and mood, including what I thought was representative (influenced by what pictures we could find) and that best told the story. Readers who disagree with the choices have every right to. There is room for debate.

The pieces came into being in the *Baltimore Jewish Times* because my late, good friend Charles "Chuck" Buerger, publisher of the *Times* from 1978 to the day he died in 1996, was enamored of the "Baltimore Glimpses" columns I had been writing for some twenty-five years for the *Baltimore Evening Sun*. Those columns examined the life and times of Baltimore in bygone days.

The *Evening Sun* folded on September 15, 1995. Chuck called me the next day and asked if I would do for the *Jewish Times* and the Jewish community what I had been doing for the *Evening Sun* and the larger Baltimore community. One did not say no to Chuck.

The result was a column in the *Times* every month for more than three years. I only wish, putting this book to bed, that I had written more pieces—there was so much going on. Saying that, I am reminded of the remark singer Helen O'Connell liked to use. When it became clear to her that many of today's younger people were interested in the big band music of their parents, she came out of retirement to do a little singing of the old stuff and to talk to the young audiences about the music. She said the kids used to shout out at her, "Tell us about the era!" Her priceless answer was *"Era*? If I had known it was going to be an *era*, I'd have paid attention."

Exactly. What follows, though, is my best shot. I owe, first of all, a debt of gratitude to all of the families and friends who lived in my old neighborhood, Cottage Avenue; I look back on my growing up among them with special fondness. Over the years of reminiscing and writing about them, my interest began to broaden, leading to the streets and the events and the institutions of the Jewish community that lay beyond. These expanded memories of Cottage Avenue led to this book.

Besides my special debt to Chuck, I am grateful to his son, Andrew, who, after the untimely death of his father, has kept up the tradition with love and loyalty. But at the core of historical writing there is research—and almost all of it for this book has been most generously supplied by Virginia North, archivist of the Jewish Museum of Maryland, and by Jeff Korman of the Enoch Pratt Library. Barry Kessler has had a hand in editing almost every word of every page of these pieces and I stand in wonderment at his editorial skills, to say nothing of his sensitivities about, and knowledge of, Baltimore Jewish history. Efrem Potts, happily for me and the record, continually challenged the accuracy of both fact and tone until we were satisfied we had it right.

The writing and the research, however, would have remained fading in old, stored copies of the *Jewish Times* had it not been for Dr. Robert J. Brugger, history editor of the Johns Hopkins University Press. The book is his idea and I am grateful to him for his confidence in me and in the work. I thank too, for gentle and knowing discipline so generously provided: Walter Sondheim, Jr., Darrell Friedman, Sarajane Greenfeld, Peggy Obrecht, Eileen O'Brien, Harry London, Bernard Fishman, Albert Berney, Barbara Katz, Michael Davis, Celestia Ward, and Dr. Solomon S. Snyder, and in absentia through their own writings, Dr. Isaac Fein and old friend Philip Kahn, Jr.

Finally, I'm grateful to all my readers who write, call, and stop me on the street—sometimes to correct me, sometimes to admonish me, even to instruct me. But more often, I'm pleased to note, it is to tell me how much they enjoy my writing and what I write about.

No writer could ask more.

Glossary for the Uninitiated

Certain Hebrew and Yiddish words and expressions occur throughout this book. The reader not familiar with them may find the following translations helpful.

Bar Mitzvah or *Bat Mitzvah*	Ceremony at age thirteen initiating a Jewish boy or girl, respectively, into the Jewish community; terms are also used for boy or girl after they have gone through the ceremony
Bubbemeise	A grandmother's tale
Cheder	Hebrew elementary school
Chumash	Five Books of Moses (Genesis, Exodus, Leviticus, Numbers, Deuteronomy)
Davening	Praying (to daven is to pray)
Gesheft	Business
Haftorah	Prophetic portion of the Prophets, the specific portion chanted by a Bar or Bat Mitzvah
Kashrut	Laws of keeping kosher according to Jewish law
Kibbutz	Collective farm or settlement (plural, kibbutzim)
Kol Nidre	A prayer chanted to a haunting melody, which ushers in the eve of the Day of Atonement and purports to nullify all vows made in innocence or under duress
Lag b'Omer	A one-day holiday between Passover and Shavuot
Mashgiach	One qualified to oversee that food and its preparation are in accordance with laws of Kashrut
Mikvah	Facility for ritual bath, or immersion, in observance of laws of family purity

Schvitz	To sweat, perspire profusely
Shabbat	The Sabbath, from Friday sundown through Saturday sundown
Shabbos Goy	A gentile doing the chores in a Jewish household on the Sabbath
Shammus	Caretaker of the synagogue
Shochet	Ritual slaughterer
Shomrei Shabbos	The custom of keeping the Sabbath in strict accordance with Orthodox Jewish law
Shtetl	A small Jewish village common in Eastern Europe
Siddur	Prayer book
Talmud Torah	Religious school in the Jewish community educational system
Torah	Scroll of the law
Tzdaka	The act of giving charity

Jewish Baltimore

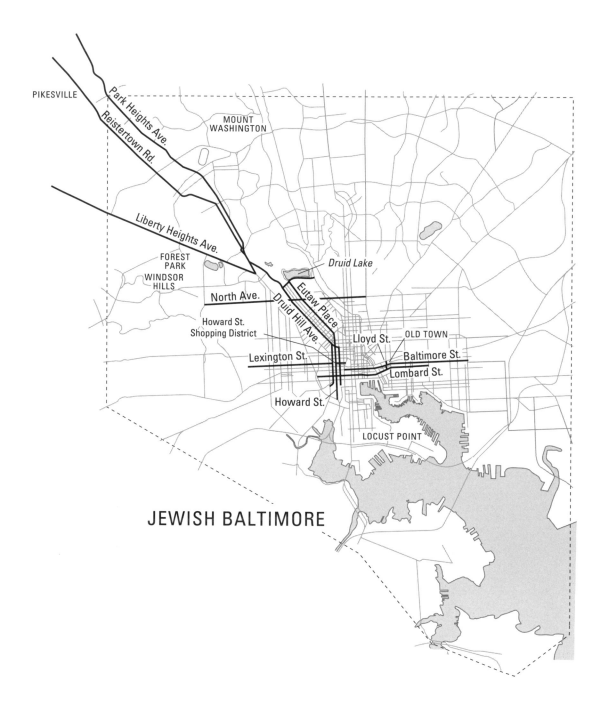

PIKESVILLE

Park Heights Ave.

Reistertown Rd.

MOUNT
WASHINGTON

Liberty Heights Ave.

FOREST
PARK

WINDSOR
HILLS

Druid Lake

Eutaw Place

North Ave.

Druid Hill Ave.

Howard St.
Shopping District

Lloyd St.

OLD TOWN

Lexington St.

Baltimore St.

Lombard St.

Howard St.

LOCUST POINT

JEWISH BALTIMORE

Prologue

Building One Community to Welcome Another

In the gray dawn of a winter's day in 1910, the passenger ship S.S. *Wilhelm* of the North German Lloyd line labored through the channel that led from the Chesapeake Bay into the Patapsco River. A long and miserable fourteen days earlier the ship had left Germany, with twelve hundred passengers bound for America. They were Jews fleeing the *shtetls*, as well as the great cities—Vilna, Kovno, Minsk, Pinsk, Kiev, Riga—of Eastern Europe. They had endured a punishing journey from Eastern Europe by railroad, by cart, and by foot to the port city of Bremen. Here, they booked passage to America. Some of the ships leaving Bremen would be going to Ellis Island (some, earlier, to Castle Garden) in New York; but the S.S. *Wilhelm* was departing for Locust Point, Baltimore.

As the S.S. *Wilhelm* came within sight of the Baltimore skyline silhouetted against a western sky, the refugees crowded the rails and jostled for position in their struggle for a first glimpse of America.

Quarantine officers had boarded the ship earlier on its way up the bay. Every immigrant had already gone through a quick and preliminary medical examination. Checking through luggage was swift and cursory. Now, there was not much to do but anticipate the end of the voyage and the beginning of a new life.

As the ship turned west passing Fort McHenry to port, the barnlike processing center at Locust Point swung into view. Hearts quickened. Within hours, exhausted, seasick, emaciated, and frightened of being sent back to an inhospitable Europe, the immigrants disembarked onto Piers 8 and 9. After endless interrogations and even more medical checks, they were free to go. Some would take the B&O Railroad to distant cities where anxious relatives awaited; others would remain and become part of Baltimore's growing and vibrant Jewish community.

"Card for Meals." Russian immigrants coming to America beginning in the 1880s were instructed to wear this card at all times while they were aboard ship, so as to be eligible for three meals a day, day one through day nineteen. Most crossings, barring storm delays, took twelve days. Note the slot that allowed card to slip over a button.

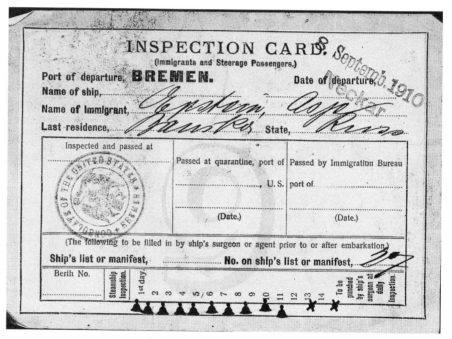

Immigrant's "Inspection Card" for Russian travelers making passage from Bremen, Germany, to Ellis Island (or, until 1892, Castle Garden), New York, or Locust Point in Baltimore. The date of departure on this card reads September 8, 1910. Immigrants came from, among many places in Central and Eastern Europe, Russia, Galicia, Lithuania, Romania, Hungary, and provinces that would become parts of Germany; and there were always a few "born at sea."

In the many retellings of this story, one will hear about other dates of arrival, other ports of entry. From 1880 to 1917 there were literally hundreds of such passages. The memories of these crossings would be passed on generation to generation. What the immigrants from Eastern Europe found in Baltimore was an organized and sophisticated Jewish community, formed along East Lombard and East Baltimore Streets between Central Avenue and the Fallsway. It was a world created by Baltimore's German Jews, themselves recent immigrants and newly come to affluence. It was to this population, and to a lesser number of earlier-arriving and progressive Eastern European Jews, that the Jewish immigrants turned when they arrived in Baltimore.

Though Jews had been living and working in Baltimore as far back as the 1780s, not until the 1830s were there enough German Jews here to gather into neighborhoods and develop a community and institutions. Some of these German Jews were not particularly happy with the influx of Russian Jews into the same city in which they themselves, through hard work and quick learning, had become "American." They made no secret of their discomfort at the ways Russian Jewish emigres dressed, talked, and worshiped. These unacculturated habits of the newer immigrants, they felt, diminished their own status and embarrassed them in front of the non-Jewish community. Still, the German Jews provided exactly what the Eastern European Jews needed—jobs. They offered employment in their flourishing manufacturing, wholesale, and retailing businesses. Generalized as "Russian Jews" even though many were from other areas in Eastern Europe, these immigrants had brought with them a talent for tailoring, and many found their way to the shops of such clothing manufacturers as L. Greif and Brother, J. Schoeneman, and Henry Sonneborn and Company. Others went to work for the retailing establishments of Hutzler's, Hochschild, Kohn, and dozens of smaller retailers and wholesalers.

As the Russian Jews found their way into East Baltimore in the decades from the 1860s into the early twentieth century, the German Jews moved out—west and north into Eutaw Place and the streets that led to it, establishing residence in the mansions and grand apartment houses that lined the boulevard. Arriving immigrants who initially could not find work soon discovered that the established Jewish community would help them find it. Not only did Jewish social services lead the immigrants to jobs, but, with an extended hand of friendship, they also provided money when and where it was needed, in particular for support until jobs could be found.

In the mid- to late nineteenth century, the Jews of Baltimore (German and Russian) formed any number of charities designed to support coreligionists in need. They included: the Hebrew Education Society (1852), the Hebrew Benevolent Society (1856), the Hebrew Hospital and Asylum (1866), the Hebrew Free Burial Society (1867), the Hebrew Orphan Asylum (1873), Daughters in Israel (1890), the Hebrew Friendly Inn and Aged Home (1890), the Milk and Ice Fund (1896), and the Hebrew Immigrant Aid Society (1903). The pattern of Jewish communal life was clear—the Jews were a tightly knit group whose members took care of one another.

Above and facing page: Immigrants at Locust Point, ca. 1904, preparing to disembark and patiently awaiting immigration-authority clearance. (Courtesy of the Peale Museum/Maryland Historical Society.)

Nonetheless, one could detect another pattern. By the 1890s Jewish Baltimore consisted of the world of the "downtown" Russian Jews (poor, immigrant) and that of the "uptown" German Jews (wealthy, Americanized). The divide persisted for at least a century.

Russian Jewish refugees who had bought into the myth that in America "the streets are paved with gold" must have been despondent at their first sight of East Baltimore. What they saw were crowded, noisy, filthy sidewalks and streets, dark and teeming tenements, and poorly dressed, sometimes foul-smelling men and women hustling merchandise—pots and pans, religious articles, or used clothing. Disheveled Yiddish-speaking vendors trafficked on the streets, on the sidewalks, out of backpacks, push-carts, and outdoor stalls. Reports of the conditions of those times and places are replete with descriptions of bad food, bad air, bad odors.

But along with this view of East Baltimore was another, shared by many: that of a community of learned rabbis, vibrant Yiddishkeit, close family life, the joys of the Jewish Educational Alliance (which offered free showers in those days of no indoor household plumbing), and the sociability offered by such institutions as Brith Sholom.

In stark contrast to the lifestyle of the "downtown" Jews, the "uptown" Jewish world was one of richly furnished mansions and apartments along Eutaw Place, itself a wide and airy boulevard of trees and gardens, flowers and fountains. These Jews lived in their own isolated and self-contained world of private clubs (one downtown on Eutaw Place, one out in the sub-

urbs with a golf course), parties, summer-long vacations, round-the-
world luxury cruises, family carriages and horses, and, in time, chauf-
feured limousines. To ensure that their children married into the right
families they created their own "coming out" and debutante parties modeled after gentile society.

The breakthrough of the Jews into Northwest Baltimore was the opening
in the early 1920s of the Shaarei Zion congregation of East European Jews
on Park Heights Avenue at Hilldale Avenue and the congregation of German Jews, Shearith Israel, much further out at Park Heights and Glen Avenues. Northwest Baltimore at the time was home mostly to gentiles. After
these two synagogues were established, many Jewish families—German
and Russian—followed; their movement into the Park Heights Avenue corridor marked the beginning of Northwest Baltimore's transformation into
a Jewish neighborhood.

Why north and west? First, the Protestant and Catholic neighborhoods
of Northeast Baltimore were not hospitable to Jews; secondly, Russian
Jews, leapfrogging up the northwest corridor, were only following in the
pattern of the German Jews, who had earlier moved out of East Baltimore to
go west and north to Eutaw Place. Whatever the reason, Jews of the old East,
South, and West Baltimore neighborhoods chose to move north and west,
and by the late 1930s Park Heights Avenue all the way to the city line was
one elongated Jewish neighborhood.

THOSE WEARY REFUGEES from Eastern Europe, peering at the skyline
of Locust Point and full of dread for the future, might have had their fears

softened if they knew they were not coming into America as "strangers in a strange land" but into a Jewish America holding out receptive arms. Baltimore's Jewish community by 1910 was over half a century old and offered a rich cultural and religious life, the largess of men of wealth, power, and influence, and an infrastructure built to take care of their own. These earlier arriving Jews were already well settled in developing neighborhoods, with both German and Russian Jews energetically working their way up the ladder of the American dream.

It was this world that the Russian-Jewish immigrants coming to Baltimore entered. In the years to come, they would become a part of the always-forming Baltimore Jewry, taking their places within it and enriching it as they changed it.

This takes us into the twentieth century and a story that leads onward and upward, even as it leads northward and westward.

The Old Neighborhood

South Baltimore: They Got off the Boat at Locust Point

Many got off the boat, got a job, and never left South Baltimore.

At the "South Baltimore Boys" reunion dinner in 1967, each guest rose to thank the "boys" for their friendship growing up in the old neighborhood; then, their parents, teachers, and mentors. They should have thanked, too, the North German Lloyd shipping line. That company had crafted the deal that helped create the South Baltimore neighborhood. Beginning in the 1860s, their ships carried passengers from Germany to Baltimore, returning to Germany with Maryland tobacco and lumber. The venue for the trade was the modest Locust Point immigration processing center at Piers 8 and 9, near South Baltimore's Fort McHenry.

The historical pattern for arriving immigrants was to take jobs quickly, close to the docks; hence, many arriving immigrants entered the waterfront life of stevedoring. But, along the lines of another historical pattern, Jews have always been drawn to the world of commerce. So it was that Jewish immigrants arriving at Locust Point beginning in the 1880s chose to bypass the waterfront jobs. It was almost a historical imperative that they would find their way to the vibrant center of Jewish life and commerce in those days, East Baltimore.

A small group of Jews who "got off the boat" at Locust Point walked up the street and got jobs in an area west of the harbor and south of Baltimore Street. They stayed, went into business, bought homes, raised families, built synagogues, and helped create the larger community that would come to be known as South Baltimore. The late Harry Shofer, one of South Baltimore's best-known figures, was fond of saying, "My family got off the boat

By the mid-nineteenth century, a lively Jewish community had emerged along East Lombard and East Baltimore Streets in the quarter east of Jones Falls. And by the mid-1870s plans were well underway for the building of Chizuk Amuno at Lloyd and Lombard Streets. H. A. Evans, Jr., painted the distinctly Moorish revival synagogue in its full glory and in its homely setting in the 1970s.

Dedicated in August 1876, it was known first as the "Friedenwald shul." Rabbi Doctor Henry Schneeberger, the first American-born ordained rabbi, served as the congregation's first rabbi. In 1895, Chizuk Amuno sold the building to the B'nai Israel congregation, which was known as the "Russiche shul." B'nai Israel congregation still functions in the restored building.

Chizuk Amuno became one of the six founding congregations of the United Synagogue of Conservative Judaism in America.

at Locust Point and we walked up to South Hanover Street. So that is where we lived for many years."

Though many Jewish families arrived in South Baltimore, relatively few remained there. Among the families who did, and who would become well known for their South Baltimore roots were the Kriegers, Shofers, Shaivitzes, Cherrys, Glicks, Samuel Shapiros, and the parents of Jacob Epstein.

As Dr. Samuel Shipley Glick recalled his family's history, his parents arrived at Locust Point in the 1890s. They settled on York Street, between Charles and Light, where the Hyatt Hotel parking lot is today. "My father," he said, "found work in a nearby cigar factory. My mother worked in the clothing lofts on Pratt Street."

As the Jewish community in South Baltimore grew, its people founded two synagogues. Both were Orthodox. The largest, Anshe Emunah, was founded in 1891 at 313 South Hanover Street, later moving to 513. The first services were held in 1894; in 1955 the congregation followed its congregants out of the city and merged into the Liberty Jewish Center. The smaller of the synagogues was Rodfe Tzedek on Hill Street near 630 South Charles Street. This synagogue closed in 1967 for lack of members and an inability to effect a merger with another congregation. The building itself was destroyed; all that remains of it is the cornerstone, now on display at the Jewish Museum of Maryland.

The Krieger family (all eight children and their parents Herman and Bettie Farber) lived in the house at 601 South Charles Street, on the corner of Lee. They were members of the Anshe Emunah synagogue. Zanvyl, born at the South Charles Street house in 1906, recalled, "My family was in the wholesale liquor business. I went to elementary school at P.S. 4 at Hanover and Lee Streets."

Henry and Lena Shofer came to Locust Point in 1904, bringing seven-year-old Harry. They moved into 626 South Hanover Street, where brothers Tom, Sam, and Reub and sisters Frieda and Minna were born and raised. Tom remembered growing up in South Baltimore: "We had no ball fields, no organized play, we kids just got together in the streets." Harry opened his first store selling bicycles at 812 South Charles Street, and then moved, switching to furniture, to 930. To this day Harry's descendants into the third generation own and operate Shofer's Furniture, in the same location at Charles and Hamburg where the family has been doing business for the better part of this century.

The Shaivitz family has long been identified with South Baltimore. Moses and Rose Shaivitz disembarked at Locust Point and settled in at 816 South Charles Street, which for a time was both the Shaivitz family home and the family furniture store. The house at 816 was where Sol and Henry and sisters Bertha and Sadie were born and raised, along with half-siblings Sylvan, Bobbie, Phyllis, and Thelma. In 1920 the Shaivitz family moved to Forest Park, where they became founders of the newly forming Beth Tfiloh synagogue.

Jacob Epstein, who became one of the wealthiest and most philanthropic of Baltimore's Jews, arrived in Baltimore in 1882 as a penniless seventeen-year-old. He opened his business at 48 West Barre Street retailing pots, pans, and clothing in South Baltimore, living over the store. That tiny business would grow to become one of the largest of its kind in America: the Baltimore Bargain House.

Mr. Epstein brought his parents, Isaac and Jennie, over to this country from Lithuania and provided homes for them in South Baltimore, at addresses that included 413 South Hanover Street and 103 West Barre Street. Isaac and Jennie were members of Anshe Emunah, at 513 South Hanover Street. Later, when they lived at 1630 McCulloh Street, they belonged to nearby Shearith Israel at 2105, where Isaac continued to worship while living as a widower at 2026.

Jacob and his wife Lena, however, were longtime members of Oheb Shalom (Rabbi William Rosenau officiated at the wedding of daughter Mar-

Interior of B'nai Israel, designed by Henry Berge and completed in 1876, at a cost of $19,810. The Ark is the work of builder and wood carver John P. Yager. Reflecting the pointed arches and other particular forms of the new Moorish style, it boasts such exotica as palm fronds carved into the decoration. The usual decalogue with old-fashioned scrollwork appears at the apex of the Ark.

ian to Sidney Lansburgh in 1910). During the years Jacob's parents lived in South Baltimore, Jennie, Jacob's mother, was active in neighborhood charities. When she died in 1911, Rabbi Elkin of Anshe Emunah officiated at her funeral and called her "the mother of charity in South Baltimore." Isaac had been president of Anshe Emunah; when he died in 1912, Rabbi Elkin, along with Rabbi Schepsel Schaffer of Shearith Israel, officiated at his funeral.

Moritz S. Shapira, who would be remembered as the father of Samuel and grandfather of Sigmund "Siggy" Shapiro, arrived in Baltimore from Taurage, Lithuania, in 1881. As Sigmund Shapiro tells the story, "He married Anna Rosenberg and they lived in South Baltimore at Sharp and Lee Streets. I remember my father saying, 'Jake Epstein was the godfather of South Baltimore. He gave everybody a job at the Baltimore Bargain House.'"

Historically, the heart of the Jewish community has been East Baltimore. But smaller Jewish communities came into being around commercial hubs within non-Jewish communities. A number of Jews lived in Hampden; others were scattered around West and Southwest Baltimore. South Baltimore was probably the largest and best known of these satellite Jewish communities. The familiar sights and sounds, streets, merchants, tiny houses, and synagogues made up a close-knit community that nurtured its residents as students, professionals, businesspeople, husbands, wives, fathers, and mothers. And as Jews.

East Baltimore: The Dream Factory

Tenements, Yiddishkeit, aspiration. . . .

There have always been two Jewish East Baltimores. The first was the East Baltimore of tenement housing, teeming streets, poverty, and the harsh life of immigrants grinding out a living. The other was the East Baltimore softened by tender reminiscence, of rich Yiddishkeit, the haunting smells of grilling hot dogs and bologna, warm rye bread, coddies and mustard, and the carnival incandescence that lit up the long-ago Saturday nights on Lombard Street.

The two East Baltimores are inseparable in the history of the Jews of Baltimore. By about 1830, East Baltimore Street between Central Avenue and the Fallsway had emerged as the largest of Baltimore's earlier Jewish neighborhoods. It was the source from which all future Baltimore Jewish neighborhoods would draw life. East Baltimore was first settled by Jews who had emigrated from the German provinces, particularly Bavaria: they arrived impoverished and began life in this country peddling clothes, umbrellas, pots and pans.

They quickly prospered, and this new-found wealth allowed them to build synagogues, where they practiced a sloppy Orthodoxy, to the dismay of their one real rabbi, Rabbi Abraham Rice. The introduction of Reform Judaism in the 1840s, with its liberating ideas on the practice of Judaism, created schisms. Many Reform Jews took off their yarmulkes, dispensed with *kashrut*, opened their stores on the *Shabbat*, and, becoming American, moved out of East Baltimore, uptown to Eutaw Place and Lake Drive. Others blended into gentile society altogether.

Historical events also hastened the move. In 1880, reacting to pogroms then sweeping Eastern Europe, waves of Jews from Eastern Europe came flooding into America. Most who arrived in Baltimore settled in East Baltimore. The neighborhood, already aging, began a dramatic change. As the Russian Jews moved in, the German Jews moved out. From these serendipitous double migrations was born the Jewish East Baltimore of fact and fancy that would be recalled through the generations in *bubbemeises*, mother to daughter, father to son. It was this Baltimore of Russian Jewish immigrants that became an American version of an Eastern European *shtetl*.

But deep within East Baltimore's mix of differing needs, motives, conflicting interests, and points of view was a singular, shared, unrelenting drive toward upward mobility, to "better oneself," to prosper beyond the level of subsistence, to shed the opprobrium of old-country "greenhorns." That is why the immigrant families turned their considerable energies to learning the language of trade and social intercourse, to mastering crafts, business, the professions, and to easing their way into mainstream America. They wanted to become comfortable with the arts, politics, and *tzedakah*. If money was scarce, aspiration was not. Sons of tailors and butchers and junkmen were encouraged to be doctors, lawyers, teachers, writers, entrepreneurs. Jewish East Baltimore was more than a neighborhood of homes and push carts and struggling storekeepers. It was a dream factory.

The Russian immigrants, often with generous help from the "uptown" German Jewish community, formed institutions that would support their desire to change rapidly and their need to hold the traditions they cherished which defined them as Jews. The Jewish Educational Alliance (JEA) is an example of the former; Brith Shalom, the night schools, Hebrew Young Men's Sick Relief, dozens of synagogues and Talmud Torahs are examples of the latter.

The JEA is probably the best remembered of all of the East Baltimore institutions. The JEA building was opened in 1914 at 1216 East Baltimore Street, a gift from the family of Michael S. Levy, whose descendants—including Lester S. Levy, Mrs. Reuben Oppenheimer, Herbert L. Moses, Leslie W. Moses—would remain associated with the JEA for years to come. According to the oral history of the JEA, its avowed purpose was "to keep

Ark of the Oheb Shalom congregation, South Hanover Street. Organized in 1853, the synagogue held its first service in Osceola Hall, Gay and Lexington Streets. In 1858 it occupied its second home (formerly the Fifth Presbyterian Church) on South Hanover Street between Pratt and Lombard Streets. The renowned Reverend Doctor Isaac M. Wise of Cincinnati officiated at the dedication. The Temple structure was rebuilt and rededicated on September 23, 1870. In 1884, the congregation celebrated the twenty-fifth anniversary of Rabbi Benjamin Szold's service as spiritual leader, and, in 1891, the same silver anniversary of the Cantor Alois Kaiser's tenure. The congregation moved in 1893 to its own building at Eutaw Place and Lanvale Street, and in 1960 it moved to 7310 Park Heights Avenue.

the children off the streets at night." The JEA itself traced its origins to the 1909 merger of the Maccabean House and the Daughters of Israel, both of which had been serving East Baltimore since the mid-1880s.

The JEA was taken over by the Associated Jewish Charities in 1925 and functioned in East Baltimore until 1951. In those years, it was a world unto itself, within which, from morning and long into the night, immigrants learned the English language (Dr. David E. Weglein, later to become super-

The de LaViez family in 1906. Samuel de LaViez left Alsace, in its time a part of both France and Germany, when he was fifteen. He met and married his wife in Leeds, England, and the couple moved again, this time to Baltimore. She died shortly afterwards. The family lived in South Baltimore, on what was once Columbus Street, where de LaViez had a hardware store. Pictured here are (*left to right*) daughter Esther, Mr. de LaViez, daughter Rose (*standing*), and sons Hirsch, Oscar, and Lee. Rose married Harry O. Levin; the couple became parents of Judge Marshall A. Levin. Hirsch became the father of Jeanne, who married lawyer and civil-rights activist Fred Weisgal.

Jeanne Weisgal explains that the use of the huge American flag as a backdrop and the two boys dressed in sailor suits is owed to Samuel's U.S. Navy service. He tended to manifest his patriotism at every opportunity. This picture was taken on the grounds of Franklin Square Hospital, on whose board of directors Mr. de LaViez served.

intendent of Baltimore City's public schools, was one of the teachers). They enjoyed concerts, lectures, dances, and plays, had the use of the print shop, took courses in stenography and business, and sent their children to the JEA's nursery and kindergarten. The facility had its own gym, which was home to legendary sports teams. There were eighty-four social clubs including the Guardians, Excelsiors, Champions, Orioles, Panthers, and Titans.

Louis Putzel was the JEA's first president. He was followed by Jose Hirsh, Fred Cone (brother of the famous art collecting Cone sisters, Claribel and Etta), and Mrs. Jacob Blaustein, who earlier, as a college student in Baltimore, had been an adviser to one of the girls' clubs. Among the alumni are Judge Simon Sobeloff, Dr. Abel Wolman, and Judge Joseph Sherbow.

Because of both the living conditions and the state of the healing arts, health care was insufficient to meet the community's needs. Tuberculosis was rampant. In 1910 almost half of those who applied to the charitable hospitals were tubercular. To serve the health care needs of the community, the Jewish communal leadership founded the Hebrew Hospital and Asylum (later Sinai Hospital) in 1868; in 1878, the Presbyterian leadership founded the Eye, Ear, and Throat Charity Hospital at 1017 East Baltimore Street. That charitable hospital has been in continuous operation in East Baltimore ever since (it now functions under management of the Greater Baltimore Medical Center). Its purpose, stated at its founding, is "to serve the suffering poor of East Baltimore." It still does.

The Jews of East Baltimore turned to the hospital for help because it was there and because if you couldn't pay you didn't have to. B. J. Small, who lived on South Eden Street near Gough Street in the 1920s, remembers going in as a young boy to have his tonsils taken out. His parents were asked. "How much can you afford to pay?" They replied, "Five dollars." The hospital's response: "Five dollars it is." Out came the tonsils.

Up through the 1950s, the 900, 1000, and 1100 blocks of old East Lombard Street were streets of legend and lore. They made up the shopping and gustatory experience that, for many, defined East Baltimore.

Mrs. Joseph Eisenberg (Frieda Faiman) lived on the 1100 block "over the store" of her father's general merchandise business. "It was a street of milling crowds, overloaded push carts, Salvation Army musicians and gypsy vans camped at Lombard and Lloyd," she recalls. "The bustle went on seven nights a week. People came from Washington and Philadelphia and stayed overnight at the nearby Turkish baths." Say "East Baltimore" today to the generation that grew up between the 1930s and the 1960s, and they immediately think of the stores and restaurants that crowded East Lombard and East Baltimore Streets: Wartzman's bakery, Saler's dairy, Yankeloff's poultry, Tulkoff's horseradish, Smelkinson's dairy, Attman's deli (still there at this writing), Holzman's bakery, Posner's kosher meats, Stone's Bakery, Sussman and Lev's deli, New York Dairy restaurant, Shulman's Roumanian restaurant.

Tobias "Toby" Hymer recalls that the very first hot dog on a roll ever sold on Lombard Street was at his father's deli, Hymer's, in the early 1930s, for three cents. "With sauerkraut," he adds, "it was four cents." No matter where one walked on the streets of East Baltimore one saw the institutions that supported its life and defined its character. On East Baltimore Street at 1012 was Brith Sholom Hall; at 1029 the Workmen's Circle Lyceum; at 1127, Sol Levinson Funeral Home (Jack Lewis Funeral Home was at 1439); at 117 North Aisquith Street was the Hebrew Friendly Inn (soon to be part of Levindale). People who lived in East Baltimore lived near a synagogue, because one had to walk to synagogue on the sabbath (riding was prohibited by Orthodox law); that is why there were so many synagogues every few blocks. Among them were: Adath B'nei Israel at 1210 East Baltimore Street (among its other addresses); Mikro Kodesh at 19 South High Street; Aitz Chaim, known as the "Eden St. Shul," at 15 South Eden Street; Shomrei Mishmeres Hakodesh at 11 Lloyd Street (in 1942); B'nai Israel (the "Russiche Shul") at 27 Lloyd Street; Anshe Neisen Nusach Ari at 16 North Exeter Street; Beth Jacob Anshe Kurland (the "Riga Kurlander Shul") at 112 North Exeter Street; and Adath Yeshurun at 127 South Exeter Street.

In the late nineteenth century, and well into the twentieth, the 900, 1000, and 1100 blocks of both East Baltimore Street and East Lombard Street hummed as retailing areas—both inside shops and on sidewalks. This typical scene along East Lombard Street—sometimes called "the Yiddish market"—dates to about 1915. Mrs. Joseph Eisenberg (Frieda Faiman) lived on East Lombard Street "over the store" of her father's general merchandise business. "It was a street of milling crowds," she recalls, "overloaded pushcarts, Salvation Army musicians, and Gypsy vans camped at Lombard and Lloyd. The hustle and bustle went on seven nights a week. People came from Washington and Philadelphia and stayed overnight at the nearby Turkish baths."

Paul Wartzman, born and raised over the family store (Wartzman's Bakery), saw these same institutions as insular, and this insularity became for him an incentive to get out. "When I was growing up, with Nathan Sefret, Sue and Ida Millstein, Marsha Zuriff, and Irv Spivak, I used to hear people who were visiting, say, at some point in their visit, that they were leaving now, to 'go home.' I thought 'Hey, I am home.' Their leaving every Saturday night to a better life elsewhere gave me an idea, to leave, too. And so I did." Mr. Wartzman grew up deep in the *shtetl* world of East Baltimore. He attended Yeshivas Chofetz Chayim (known also as the "Parochial school"). For movies, he went to the nearby Cluster, State, and Broadway Theaters; for "medical care" he walked into the nearest pharmacy, in his case, Flom's at Baltimore and Wolfe Streets.

Seymour Attman (at this writing) still works at Attman's on East Lombard Street, although he doesn't live there anymore. "But," he notes, "I carry with me, as do all who lived in East Baltimore, the memory of being in want. Of things we take for granted today. Like heat. It's a good thing in life to have lived in East Baltimore and to have known want."

Miriam Greenberg (Mrs. Pat Paperman) was born on Ann Street but moved to 1826 East Fairmount Avenue. She went to elementary school at P.S. 97 at Fairmount and Ann Streets, then to Junior High at P.S. 40 on

Aisquith Street. She and her girlfriends Blanche Needle and Thelma Bleich often walked to the Cluster and the Broadway Theaters, then to Malin's deli at Baltimore and Ann Streets, sometimes to Flom's Pharmacy "for the best milkshakes in the world." They took part in plays and public speaking contests at the JEA's Emanon Club. "It was a happy time because we didn't know we were poor," she says. "We didn't have skates or dolls or bicycles. Our parents would give us a choice: 'You want a pickle, or an ice cream? What?'"

Winds of change blew through East Baltimore in the late 1930s and seemed to take the immigrants' dream factory with them. The neighborhood's transformation from a familiar *shtetl* into a museum of memories was breathtakingly quick. Baltimore's Jewish community has since moved on, in an ever quickening odyssey that has taken it far—geographically, culturally, economically, socially. Along the way, old East Baltimore, with its storied commerce and culture and ethos, needs to be remembered. It was, after all, the point of departure.

The Baths of Old East Baltimore: In a Time before Indoor Plumbing

"For a nickel, you are sovereign."

The *Standard Jewish Encyclopedia* notes: "Bathing has always been important to Jews. Physical cleanliness was cultivated because, as Hillel taught, the body is the receptacle that holds the soul. Bathing on Fridays in honor of the approaching Sabbath was almost universal in Judaism."

The Jews who came over to this country from Eastern Europe and settled in East Baltimore brought with them the tradition of bathing to prepare for the Sabbath. That is why, up to the mid 1950s, in honor of the approaching Sabbath on Friday afternoons, many of East Baltimore's men (not women, however) would head for Central Avenue and Lombard Street to join friends and family and take the baths in Magid's or one of the many other public or private ("Turkish") baths popular in East Baltimore in those days. Some were privately owned, like Magid's, Sanitary Russian Baths at 1427 East Baltimore Street, and New York Russian Baths at 116 East Baltimore Street. The six public baths were called Walters' Baths, after their benefactor, Henry Walters of art museum fame.

Jerry Schloss recalled his Friday afternoon visits to Magid's. "They'd rub you down, then you'd sit in the steam room. All around the wall there were maybe four tiers of seats, one higher than the next. The higher you got, the hotter it got."

An East Baltimore alley in 1916. Besides serving as playgrounds for the children, alleys were also junk men's primary hunting grounds. The junk men of old East Baltimore, some of whom became the giants in the rag and scrap metal businesses, later reminisced about scouring these alleys with shoulder packs and stuffing them with rags, shards of metal, and bottles. (Courtesy of the Maryland Historical Society.)

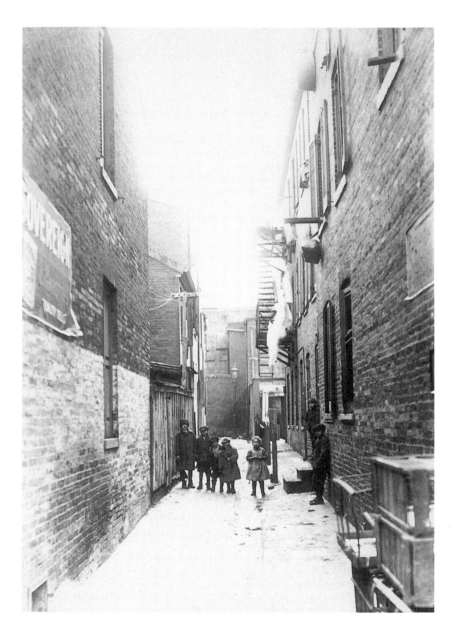

The most popular public bathhouse was at 131 South High Street, Walters' No. 1. In 1951 almost 50,000 persons took sanctuary in this warm and watery haven. Among them was William Manchester of the *Evening Sun*, on his way to prominence as newspaperman and author.

Mr. Manchester arrived shortly after nine on a fine June morning, paid five cents to get in (towel and soap came with the price of admission), and another five cents for a comb. "Each shower," he later wrote, "has its own dressing room, hooks for clothes, a slate seat, and a slotted door which locks for privacy. For a nickel you are sovereign. "I dried myself on a stiff towel marked 'Baltimore City Bath Commission. 1950. 50th Year.' And I came out like the name on the soap wafer they gave me when I went in—'Beauty White.'"

Reminiscences and newspaper accounts of the 1920s through the 1950s suggest that Baltimoreans at every level of business, government, and academe, well beyond the East Baltimore neighborhood, visited the baths. Among the regulars were Daniel Willard, president of the B&O Railroad; Moses Rothschild, president of Sun Life Insurance; Jacob Epstein, millionaire philanthropist and founder of the Baltimore Bargain House; and William Welch, famed Johns Hopkins pathologist and one of the "Big Four" who founded the university's medical school. Pulling himself out of an ice cold pool, Welch was heard to remark, "Something about these Turkish baths. They give you all the benefits of exercising without the nuisance of it."

Solomon Liss, a well-known raconteur, lawyer, and Baltimore City Councilman, reminisced about his experience with the public baths of East Baltimore:

Our home had a cast iron bathtub with a porcelain finish. It sat upon four cast iron legs with clawed feet. It served its purpose as a private bath, but it had no shower. Once a week I was permitted to go to the bathhouse. There I paid a nickel to the attendant seated behind a small window. This bought me a towel similar to the face towels used in barbershops, wrapped around a small slice of soap. I took my place on one of the benches around the wall of the outer room and awaited my turn.

When somebody called out "Next!" I was ushered into a room lined on each side by half a dozen shower stalls. Each stall had a small square of slate above the latch and on this slate the attendant chalked the time as I entered the stall.

A quick disrobing and then the adjustable faucets could be regulated to provide a spread of temperatures ranging from the heat of Hades to the cold of the Arctic. Singing was permitted and all of us gave the popular harmonies of the day a good workout.

Time was easily forgotten and most bathers had to be brought back to reality by the attendant's banging on the door to remind them that they had "one more minute." At the end of his time it was not unusual for a patron to be ushered briskly out of the shower room, rinsed off or not, clothes under his arm, into the dressing room nearby. The fresh, buoyant experience on my re-entry into the outside world is even today indescribable.

By the mid-1950s indoor plumbing had extended into practically all Baltimore houses. With the Health Department rule that every habitable residence must contain a bathtub or shower, it became clear that the days of the public baths were numbered. In 1956 we in the City Council, under pressure as always to economize, approved the closing of the public baths. In the process a lot of nostalgic farewells were expressed.

An anecdote making the rounds in those days was that A. H. S. (for Alexander Hamilton Stump) Post, then president of Mercantile Safe Deposit and Trust, had met Daniel Willard outside a Turkish bath one day and cautioned him against taking too many baths.

"They are, Dan, too much of an exertion for a man your age," said Mr. Post.

Mr. Willard, fresh out of the bath and feeling exhilarated, responded sternly. "Friends of mine have been telling me that for fifteen years. I must tell you most of them are dead."

Mr. Willard may have been right about the baths. He lived to eighty-one.

Right and facing page: The Snesil family lived at 2101 East Baltimore Street, not far from the dairy that Moses and Louis, father and son, owned at 1050 Granby Street. They sold bottled milk door-to-door through the streets of East Baltimore from horse-drawn wagons. *Left to right:* Becky Snesil (daughter); Moses Snesil; Louis Snesil (son); Rose Snesil; and Sarah Snesil (daughter).

ON DECEMBER 29, 1959, the last of the public bathhouses was scheduled to be shut down. It was Walters' No. 2 at 900 Washington Boulevard. Closing was set for five that afternoon.

At five minutes to five there was still one man left in the shower. The attendant for twenty-seven years, George Price, was stacking the towels for the last time. He knew that when this last patron in these closing minutes came out of the shower it would be the end. When the patron did emerge, unmindful that he had soaped himself into history, he turned out to be a man in his eighties. He wore a woolen shirt and dungarees and carried a shopping bag in which he had stuffed his used clothing. Price told him as he left that his visit was the last, and as such, historic. The bather's response did not reflect commensurate awe. He snapped, "Where are poor people supposed to go to take a bath?"

In each of the bathhouses there was a guest book for patrons to sign and to comment on the service. One wrote, "In the rooming houses the first in the bath gets all the hot water. The last gets none. Here there's hot water all the time." And another wrote this last comment in the last operating bathhouse in Baltimore: "It's a Godsend!"

Henrietta Szold: Teacher, Pioneer, Visionary

The explanation for the grandeur of her dreams lies in Baltimore.

America and the world know Henrietta Szold as the courageous Jewish woman who invigorated the Zionist movement in America, gave it much of its vision, and helped ensure its perpetuity. But the Baltimore Jewish community knows her best as one of their own. Born in Baltimore in 1860, the daughter of Rabbi Benjamin Szold, the renowned rabbi of Temple Oheb Shalom, she grew up on Lombard Street in the patrician German Jewish world of which her father was so much a part. She graduated from Western High School, and for some fifteen years taught French, German, and mathematics at a girls' high school, as well as classes at Temple Oheb Shalom. But through it all, the heart of this sensitive and restless young woman was drawn to help the poor Russian immigrants arriving in East Baltimore by the thousands. Her personal mission was to instill the spiritual in American Judaism, which she felt had been lost in the immigrants' relentless pursuit of material wealth.

Her involvement with a group of young, intellectual immigrants took her to a leadership role in the founding in 1889 of what came to be known as "the Russian Night School" in East Baltimore. The school became a model for the Americanization of immigrants. At the first class in rented spaces in a corner of the immigrant ghetto (Gay Street near Front Street), only thirty newcomers, both men and women, attended. But the very next evening a second class was formed. And soon a third; one hundred and fifty adults were taught during the first year. The school flourished beyond the dreams of Miss Szold and her society's members.

At the same time, Miss Szold's search for ideas to strengthen Jewish life led her to become active in the movement to establish a Jewish homeland in Palestine. In 1903, at age forty-three, she left Baltimore for New York to study at the Jewish Theological Seminary. Following a trip to Palestine in 1909, she became active in the Hadassah Study Circle, a women's Zionist group, and a few years later she was the driving force that transformed that group into the first chapter of the Women's Zionist Organization, whose mission was to improve health conditions in Palestine. Hadassah grew into the largest Zionist organization in America.

In 1920, at age sixty, Miss Szold moved to Palestine. There, for the next three years, she directed the Hadassah Medical Organization. In 1927 she was elected by the Zionist Congress as a member of the Zionist Executive, responsible for health and education, the first woman to hold such a position. From 1934 Miss Szold committed her considerable energy and administrative skills to Youth Aliyah, an organization concerned with the plight of Jewish youth in Europe. Youth Aliyah, funded in large part by Hadassah, helped thousands of children escape the Holocaust.

Henrietta Szold died of pneumonia in 1945 in Jersusalem, at the Hadassah School of Nursing, which she had helped bring into being.

HENRIETTA SZOLD'S NAME and work became a part of world history. But when biographers search for the roots of her inspiration, her commitment to social justice, and her zeal for her faith. they must come to Baltimore. Here they will find the explanation for the grandeur of her dreams.

East Lombard Street scenes, 1920s. In a Sunday feature piece in 1924, the *Sun* described the 1100 block as having all "the colorful atmosphere of an Old World marketplace, bearded men with baskets, old Orthodox Jewish women with shawls and wigs."

THE SUN

BALTIMORE, SUNDAY MORNING, APRIL 13, 1924

altimore Has A Colorful Old-World M

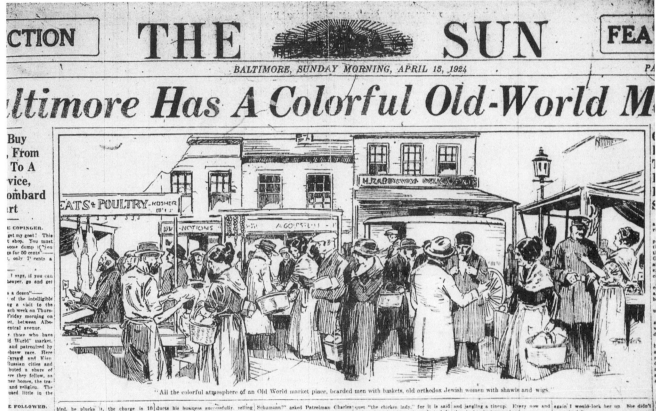

"All the colorful atmosphere of an Old World market place, bearded men with baskets, old orthodox Jewish women with shawls and wigs."

Above and facing page: Welcoming window and pickle-barrel-lined carryout counter of Sussman's deli, 923 East Baltimore Street. In 1926, the business became Sussman and Lev's. An early menu offered lox and cream cheese, spiced beef, corned beef, roast beef, salami, chopped liver, and combinations of some or all of these, along with an invitation to wash it all down with an Almond Smash soda. Believed to be the first full-scale Baltimore deli (it closed in the mid-1950s), Sussman and Lev's was followed by many others, including Ballow's, Nates and Leon's, Awrach and Perl's, Mandell-Ballow's, Weiss's, Attman's, Kessler's, Cooper's, and Lapides's.

In 1935 Sussman and Lev expanded, adding
this art-deco bar, a ceramic-tile floor, and
table booths. The deli also imported a Vien-
nese baker via New York City. In 1939 the
restaurant offered air conditioning and in-
stalled a catering hall upstairs.

Left: Advertisement for "Sussman and Lev" deli as it appeared in Yiddish, in the Baltimore edition of the *Jewish Daily Forward*, September 12, 1952. Only address and phone numbers (Mulberry 6321 and Saratoga 5358) appeared in English.

Above: Chickens flutter in crates piled on East Lombard Street sidewalks, a common sight until the mid-1970s. Progress in public health ended the longstanding practice whereby customers, after some haggling with the seller, carefully selected a chicken from the crate and ordered it killed on the spot.

Above and facing page: East Lombard Street, 1963 (*left*) and 1967 (*right*). From the delicatessens, bakeries, fruit, and poultry stalls came the heady and haunting aromas of hot dogs, salami and mustard, homemade pickles in strong brine (bay leaves, ginger, cloves), freshly cut onions, ground peppers, and rye bread still warm. (Though there were also odors of rotting fruit, chicken blood, and horse manure.) The food stores in the street's glory days included Wartz- man's bakery, Smelkinson's dairy, Pastore's fruits and vegetables, Tulkoff's horseradish, Yankeloff's chickens, Attman's deli, Holz- man's bakery, Spivak's chickens, Gottlieb's dairy, and Stone's bakery. In the spring of 1968, following the assassination of the Rev- erend Martin Luther King, Jr., many of these buildings gave way to empty lots. (1967 pho- tograph, *facing page*, courtesy of the *Balti- more Sun.*)

Bill Wilson's 1990s sketch of the famous 1000 block of East Lombard Street makes up in romance what it lacks in accuracy. It is difficult, indeed, to get the scene down on paper: The mix of people, languages, and shops; the bustle of sidewalk life spilling out into the streets; the clash of cultures—old, young, rich, poor, Jews and non-Jews from diverse backgrounds—all came together in both harmony and discord in a nineteenth-century urban experience. A challenge too large for even the talented pen of Mr. Wilson! (Courtesy of William "Bill" Wilson.)

The Private World of German Jewry

The Phoenix Club: Baltimore German Jewish Society's First Home

The German Jews opened a society, closed it, then lost it.

The term *Jewish society* has always been suspect. The words seem to be in contradiction. *Society* has been defined through centuries of American life as a matter of family, country of origin, and wealth. Up to the mid-nineteenth century, when the issue of a Jewish society was of interest to them, Baltimore's Jews could lay little claim to any of these criteria. They had not been in this country very long; their own country of origin had no particular standing in American society; and in terms of wealth, Baltimore's German Jews had not built fortunes at the level of, say, New York's "Our Crowd" of Guggenheims, Seligmans, Loebs, Lehmans, Goldmans, Sachses, and Kuhns.

By the mid- to late nineteenth century a number of Baltimore's German Jewish families had gained social stature by virtue of their growing wealth and leadership in the charities. In the Jewish community, at any rate, it seemed that originating from a country of Western Europe was considered more prestigious than originating from Eastern Europe. Retailing, wholesaling, and the manufacturing of clothing had provided many Western European Jews who had immigrated earlier with undreamed of wealth. An exclusive in-town club in which they could share life at a certain social stratum soon became a need waiting to be filled. And to intensify the need, Russian Jews, with distinctly "old world" language and lifestyles, were now flooding into Baltimore and threatening the Germans' newly won status as "Americans." Many German Jews felt the need to separate themselves from this "too Jewish" tide of immigrants.

So it was, on February 7, 1886, as the club's minutes read, "a small group

At the "Executive Table." On January 23, 1882, the Hebrew Hospital and Asylum (later Sinai Hospital) sponsored a fundraising "Grand Charity Ball" at the Academy of Music, then at Howard and Franklin Streets. This announcement in the program identified representatives present from the hospital, the Hebrew Orphan Asylum, and the Harmony Circle. Among the representatives were David Hutzler, Levi Greif, Leopold Strouse, and Robert Austrian.

of men met at the office of Martin Lehmayer at 51 Lexington Street for the purpose of formally organizing a literary and social club. Mr. Andrew Saks was elected as temporary presiding officer." Other members of the officer slate, board, and organizing committee included Hiram Wiesenfeld, Henry L. Straus, Simon Dalsheimer, and David Hutzler. The club rented the Johnson Building at 118 Park Avenue for its clubrooms, but by 1891 it was able to move into its own extravagant quarters at 1505 Eutaw Place. For the first time, Baltimore's Jewish society had a home. And it would be these founding members of the Phoenix Club, and their children after them, who would be that society's tastemakers for the next half century in this closed circle of friendship and fancy.

The red sandstone building was three and a half stories tall. The interior was designed to be gracious, open, light, and airy. Its spacious rooms were often the scene of the German Jewish society's most important social functions, including the Harmony Circle debutante balls. The millionaire philanthropist Jacob Epstein (from Lithuania) met his friends here to play pinochle. (The German-only membership policy was situational; wealth, philanthropy, and prominence in certain cases outweighed "country of origin.") After their game they could visit downstairs and enjoy the billiard room, bowling alley, and barber shop.

The sitting room on the first floor, with its comfortable chairs and dim lighting, was in the tradition of the more elegant New York German Jewish men's clubs. Silence was the inflexible rule. On February 5, 1925, however, the tranquility was shattered by an incident the likes of which the members hoped they would never see again. According to a report in the *Sun*, Emanuel Hecht, of the Hecht Company department store empire, collapsed and died in the Phoenix Club "where he was spending the afternoon with friends." After a luncheon at his home at 1739 Eutaw Place, Mr. Hecht had left for the club. Shortly after, at about 3:00 P.M., he was found dead on the floor. Dr. Louis P. Hamburger was in attendance. The unfortunate death did not appear to affect life at the club. It went on.

The schedule of events for October through December 1945 included stags, bingo nights, open ballroom dances, "Blue Room" dances, the Thanksgiving Cocktail Dance, and, of course, the very gala New Year's Eve ballroom dance. Former member Arthur Gutman says, "The biggest event of the Phoenix Club social season was the Masquerade Ball. It was lots of fun and everybody you knew was there—behind a mask."

Leonard Greif and his wife, Ann Burgunder Greif, were regulars at the club in the years leading up to their marriage, in 1940, and beyond. Mr. Greif recalls, "We went there most every Saturday night. It was a way of life. There was always a dance with a leading orchestra, Jack Lederer's orchestra for one. The dancing was always reserved and on the dignified side— ballroom dancing for the most part. Also among those who were regulars were Mary Louise Fleischmann Gutman, Sidney Lansburgh, Jr., and Kaufman Katz." Some observers opined that the club's society life was designed to emulate the gentile society life.

While many of the members remember the club for its amenities, others recall its unapologetic exclusiveness. According to Mr. Gutman, who was an active member from the early 1930s to the club's closing in 1969, "In its early years, few Jews who were not of German extraction were admitted. The truth is, the club was about the people in it. In those days you had to be somebody to get in. The blackball system of turning down applications was used often."

In 1945 the initiation fee was fifty dollars, and dues of one hundred dollars each year were required to sustain membership.

The minutes list earlier presidents: from 1886 through 1905, Andrew Saks, Lewis Lauer, Samuel Rosenthal, Matthew Keyser, Albert A. Brager, Louis Gutman, Max Hochschild, Leon C. Coblens, and Julian S. Stein. The family names that helped make up the membership list of the Phoenix Club in the first decades of the twentieth century were the same family names that made up the membership lists of the Suburban Club into the 1930s and of the Harmony Circle Ball debutante "coming out parties" of the 1920s and

1930s—Hutzler, Berney, Sondheim, Burgunder, Lansburgh, Hecht, and Rothschild, to name just some. The founders of the Phoenix Club had succeeded in their mission; they had opened the circle, and then closed it.

Barbara Pollock Katz, from a much later generation, has her own memories of the Phoenix Club:

> My grandfather, Morris Schapiro, played cards there, pinochle I am sure, most every Saturday all through the 1940s and early 1950s. I went to dinner with the family there often. When Jay and I were married in December of 1953 his Uncle Cal Zamoiski, with his son Calman "Buddy" Zamoiski and Buddy's wife Ellen Levi Zamoiski, gave us a lovely luncheon there after our wedding rehearsal.
>
> My high school sorority, Sigma Theta, had its annual Snowball Dance every Christmas Eve at the Phoenix Club. They were beautiful affairs, all tuxedoes and formal gowns. Among our members were Joan Green Klein, Sarah Offit Abeshouse, and Phyllis Cahn Finkelstein. I can't remember any of the guys except this one date of mine—Harvey Kayne.

Eutaw Place: Jewish, but Not "Too Jewish"

The "Champs Élysées of Baltimore" was a street of Jewish patrician life.

Eutaw Place was born to the purple. The boulevard up until World War II had known only the homes of the wealthy, for whom it had been created. It was originally laid out in 1817 as a sixty-six-foot-wide extension of Eutaw Street, then known as Gibson Street.

By the mid-1850s, American cities were competing with one another in the development of architecture and landscaping. Baltimore's city fathers got caught up in the fever; they retained an architect to plan a grand boulevard in Baltimore, one whose splendor would rival that of the Champs Elysees in Paris. To provide the land for it, the city bought up all of the old country estates on what became Eutaw Place.

Ordinary-looking Gibson Street was widened, and a landscaped median strip was built from Dolphin Street to North Avenue. In 1854, the name was changed to Eutaw Place, after Eutaw, South Carolina, a battle site where John Eager Howard had won fame during the Revolutionary War. By 1896, Eutaw Place was a broad and lovely avenue of fountains and plants and promenades, its twelve blocks from Dolphin Street to Lake Drive a ribbon of elegance.

Many of the homes were built large, for it was an era of expansiveness. Families were big and household staffs of five or more were not unusual. Homes were built well, too, for technological advances in mill and foundry work had extended the artistry of craftsmen and allowed for a higher level of building and ornamentation.

Some of Baltimore's best-known families lived in these mansions: the Isaac Emersons (of the same "Captain Emerson" who invented Bromo Seltzer, owned Emerson Farms, and built the Emersonian apartments and the old Emerson Hotel), the McCormicks (of spice fame), Van Lear Blacks (of the *Sunpapers*), Dr. William Halstead and Dr. William Kelly (both of the Hopkins "Big Four"), Dr. J. M. T. Finney, the Snowdens, the Mallorys, and the Booths.

A Sunday stroll would take in the magnificent Centennial Fountain in the 1600 block and the Francis Scott Key monument in the median strip at

The Phoenix Club, 1505 Eutaw Place, in 1910. Its founders in 1886 aimed to establish an institutional or formal expression of German Jewish society, and they succeeded. Located in the heart of the Eutaw Place German Jewish community, the club flourished as a convenient in-town gathering spot.

Lanvale Street, designed by Jean M. A. Marcie, with Tuscan columns and a heroic bronze of the Maryland poet and author of the "Star Spangled Banner." But by the 1880s, quietly, subtly, as neighborhoods do in an upwardly mobile society, Eutaw Place had begun to change. The old families moved out: the Jews were coming.

Newcomers were of the merchant and professional class, families who had enjoyed economic success and were now moving out of East and West Baltimore and up the ladder of the American dream. By the turn of the century the Jewish families whose standing and wealth created the aura of elegance associated with a Eutaw Place address were well ensconced there.

Flora Thalheimer, Ida Gutman, Moses Rothschild, and Moses Kahn lived in the Esplanade; the Friedenwalds lived at 1212 Eutaw Place; the Westheimers lived in the Emersonian, as did Ansel Schoeneman and Max Hochschild. Claribel and Etta Cone lived in the Marlborough, as did Ira Fader and Jay Strouse. The Hutzlers lived at 1801 at the corner of Laurens; above North Avenue, the Jacob Engels lived at 2422; Moses Hecht was at 2442; David Greif at 2510; Jerome Benesch at 2430.

According to the oral history of the community, the culture of the German Jews of Eutaw Place was distinctly German. Many were members of the Concordia German Society, and the Concordia Opera House was the center of their social activities. Some were active in German charities and participated in German musical societies and literary clubs. It was common for German to be spoken in family life and taught to the children.

Eutaw Place as a separate enclave began to fade as early as the mid-1930s, and the process was about complete by the 1960s. A combination of factors led to this: the acute housing needs created by World War II (which were satisfied in part by cutting the Eutaw Place mansions into many separate apartments), the forces of suburbanization, the intermarrying of German and Eastern European Jews, and the growing wealth and stature of many Eastern European Jews. By the beginning of the 1970s, few German Jews were living on Eutaw Place. They had moved to Mt. Washington and Upper Park Heights along with Eastern European Jews, as the lines between the two cultures began to blur.

Five Apartment Houses on Eutaw Place: Citadels of Prestige

Today it is debatable which apartment houses offer the most prestigious addresses and carry the most luminous cachet for Baltimore Jews. But until the mid-1950s there could be no argument. The distinction belonged

These five apartment houses on Eutaw Place made up a German Jewish community of affluence.

to five apartment buildings in the Eutaw Place–Lake Drive area: the Esplanade, the Emersonian, Temple Gardens, the Marlborough, and the Riviera. These were the addresses that, in the Jewish community, meant wealth, power, influence, and family name. They also meant country of origin; the residents were for the most part Jews who traced their roots to German-speaking areas of Europe.

When the Riviera opened in May 1915, newspaper stories were ecstatic in their praise: the *Sun* placed it "among Baltimore's handsomest and most costly of apartment houses." Located on the southwest corner of Lake Drive and Linden Avenue, the Riviera offered a stunning view of Druid Hill Park Lake. Each unit had ten-foot-high ceilings, a glass-enclosed porch that could be converted into a conservatory, and a separate maid's entrance. Tenants included Abraham Cahn, Mrs. Albert Hecht, Henry Laupheimer, Henry Frank, Nelson Gutman, Robert Kerngood, Alexander Hecht, Leonard Greif, Samuel Thalheimer, Mrs. Theresa Burgunder, Aaron Benesch, and Samuel Hamburger.

The Esplanade was completed in 1915. Among the residents were Flora Thalheimer, Jay Himmelrich, Henry Burgunder, Simon Dalsheimer, Sadie Gutman, Herman Kerngood, Moses Rothschild, Emma Thalheimer, Samuel Kann, Reuben Ottenheimer, Tema Zamoiski, Adolph Sinsheimer, Louis Berney, Jacob Gomprecht, and Rabbi William Rosenau.

The Emersonian was built in 1916 by Captain Isaac Emerson. Residents included Max Hochschild, Louis Blaustein, Sydney Westheimer, Minnie Wiesenfeld, Moses Strouse, Sidney Thanhouser, Ansel Schoeneman, and Ferdinand Neuberger. Temple Gardens was built in 1925; tenants included the families of Jerome Kahn, Theodore Newhoff, and Florence Gutman.

The Marlborough, built in 1906 at 1707 Eutaw Place, was home to: in apartment 10A, the Henry Hamburgers; in 3B, Ida Oppenheimer; 7J, Olga Grinsfelder; and in 8B, Claribel Cone. In this apartment, Claribel, her sister Etta, and her brother Fred had assembled some of the world's most valuable works of art, including works by Matisse, Picasso, and Gauguin.

Why were these residences mostly German Jewish? The social and economic history of Baltimore makes that clear. These families arrived in Baltimore beginning in the 1840s, mostly from Bavaria. Settling in East Baltimore, they became quite successful from peddling, manufacturing, wholesaling, and retailing. Suddenly they were rich in wealth and status, all within twenty years or so. But following a deeply-ingrained pattern in American society—when the poor move in, the rich move out—the German Jews who were enjoying success in their businesses moved out of East Baltimore, migrating "uptown" to Eutaw Place and Lake Drive. In the Eutaw

With its development in the 1880s, Eutaw Place became more than an address. For Baltimore's German Jewry it was a way of life. Modeled after the Champs Élysées in Paris, it offered wide vistas, water fountains, winding paths, and flower gardens. Residents included wealthier German Jewish families—Hechts, Greifs, Hutzlers, Beneschs. This picture of the median strip was taken in 1881; Eutaw Place's prestige began to fade by the 1930s. (Courtesy of the Maryland Historical Society.)

Place—Lake Drive community they founded their own separate society, with an in-town club (the Phoenix Club), a country club (the Suburban Club), and their own funeral home (the Sondheim Funeral Home).

The homes along Eutaw Place were built to accommodate large families and staffs of servants. Understandably, then as now, as the residents grew older and their children moved away, they shied from the responsibilities of maintaining such large homes and sought apartments in the same neighborhood, near family, friends, and Reform temples. Builders, sensing the demand, were quick to meet it. Beginning in 1915, German Jews who had been living in the mansions of Eutaw Place and Lake Drive found these five very attractive apartment houses waiting for them.

Donald Kann was born and raised in the Esplanade and lived in apartment 6c until he was six years old. His parents were Louis M. Kann, Jr., and Frances Ottenheimer Kann; his maternal grandparents were members of the Gomprecht and Benesch families, shareholders in the Maryland Land

and Investment Corporation—the business that built and operated the building. When Donald Kann reached school age, he and best friend Neal Meyers attended P.S. 234, Arlington Elementary, compliments of the Baltimore City School System, which provided a little yellow bus to pick them up and take them home every school day. Mr. Kann recalled: "I have a continuous memory as an infant playing with John Katz and Jimmie Wertheimer on the lawn between the Esplanade and Lake Drive, where it abuts the Hendler property. We hauled our bikes up and down the elevators. Friday night was the big night. Every apartment must have had fifteen or twenty people for dinner."

These German Jews were not only in the same businesses and living in the same neighborhood, but in many cases they were also related. And all seem to have had a member of the family living in one of the apartment-house citadels of Baltimore's German Jewish aristocracy.

A look at the leadership of the Associated Jewish Charities, the larger business establishments, the directors of the Suburban Club, and the tenants of the Esplanade, Temple Gardens, the Emersonian, the Marlborough, and the Riviera of those days shows that certain family names keep reappearing: the Kohns, Hutzlers, Hechts, Greifs, Schoenemans, Sonneborns, Strouses, Westheimers, Dalsheimers, Franks, and Laupheimers.

The German Jews' status kept them distant from the larger Jewish world; socially, they kept to themselves. But one could always find them most any Friday night at their family dining room tables in the Esplanade, Temple Gardens, Emersonian, Riviera, and the Marlborough.

You won't find them there any more. This community of myth and memory, as well as the concentration of wealth, family, influence, and upscale address that once confirmed its status, has melted away. The storied apartment buildings are today host to tenants of diverse backgrounds, economic status, and religious affiliation. The homogenous group of occupants who gave the buildings their aura of privilege until around 1960 are now but one more part of the larger, multifaceted population we call Baltimore's Jewish community.

Becoming American: German Jewish Debutantes' "Harmony Circle Balls"

In the history of Baltimore Jewry the so-called uptown Jews (read "German") and the downtown Jews ("Russian") had many differences but shared one common aspiration: to become "American" as quickly as possible. The downtown Russian Jews pursued the dream by studying the new language and learning trades that would afford them the opportunity to move up socially and economically. East Baltimore, with its schools and its clubs and its classes, became a university of the people.

But by the 1880s, when the Russian Jews began arriving in Baltimore in large numbers, the German Jews had already learned the language and mastered the trades and were moving out of East Baltimore and into the then-suburban and tonier Eutaw Place. They pursued the dream by adopting aspects of the lifestyle of Anglo-America, one of which was the Protestants' debutante balls. The German Jewish establishment, duplicating this tradition, sponsored Jewish versions of it so that, in the same Protestant tradition, daughters of the right families could meet sons of the right families.

These German Jewish debutante balls in Baltimore were known as the Harmony Circle Balls. Predictably, as the German Jews borrowed the institution, they also borrowed the mainstream rationale for it—charity. Proceeds of the balls were contributed to institutions in East Baltimore to support the Russian Jews in their struggle to Americanize. To name some of the charities (but surely not all): the Hebrew Benevolent Society, the Ladies Sewing Circle, the Hebrew Hospital and Asylum, and the Hebrew Orphan Asylum.

With music, taffeta, and flowers, German Jewish society created a world of its own.

ON WEDNESDAY EVENING, November 29, 1929, something very big was happening on Chase Street between Charles and St. Paul Streets. Outside the entrance of the Belvedere Hotel was a churning scene of limousines and bright lights, taffeta, tuxedos, flowers, music, and picture-taking. On the street, on the sidewalk, there were polite introductions and warm embraces.

The stock market had crashed only a few weeks earlier, setting off the Depression and sending the country into despair, but there was no hint of any of that here. For Baltimore's German Jews, this event was the time and the place to see and be seen. It was the Seventieth Annual Harmony Circle Ball. The next day, the *Sun*, falling over itself to capture the social significance of the night, emoted: "13 Debutantes Bow Socially in Harmony Circle Fairyland."

The scene did indeed appear to be a fairyland, or as close to one as the managers of the event, known as governors, could make it. Among these governors were James Levi, Charles Weiler, Eli Frank, and Lewis Hess. If we are to believe the *Sun*'s description of the decor, the governors did their work well.

"An attractive note was given to the story of Cinderella, when a pageant, directed by Mrs. Adelaide Gutman Nathan, was presented, with debutantes as members of the cast, called the 'Dance of the Decades.' The pageant depicted in eight episodes the evolution of the dance from the founding of the Harmony Circle in 1860 to the present." The story went on to list the debutantes making their debut: Miss Rosalie Hecht, daughter of Mr. and Mrs. Leonard Hecht, Escort, Joseph Hecht. ("Miss Hecht wore cream colored tulle over satin, appliqued with panne velvet. Chaperoned by Mrs. Hecht, attired in an amethyst taffeta gown and slippers to match.")

Other debutantes introduced at that same ball and similarly described were Miss Jane T. Hutzler, Miss Vivian J. Berman, Miss Dorothy Jandorf, and Miss Rose Helen Hamburger. An ambiance reminiscent of F. Scott Fitzerald's novels prevailed in the ballroom. The walls were hidden behind curtains of gold cloth; draperies of the same material flanked the long windows. Golden vases containing autumnal fruits and flowers were placed at intervals along the walls, and garlands of flowers were draped from the balcony.

The report continued: "To appropriate music, a golden coach was driven into the ballroom by Messrs. Kahn, Goldstein, Strouse, Cohen, Wolf, and Levi. Sigmund Spaeth, writer of the music, held the reins and after the coach had circled the room he played his own accompaniment at the piano where he sang ballads telling the story of the Harmony Circle from the founding in 1860 to the present."

The first Harmony Circle Ball was held on October 16, 1860, at Old Oak Hall in East Baltimore. Formed originally as a dancing society for the children of the wealthier German Jews, the group very soon became known as the Harmony Circle. The founding officers elected at that meeting were Louis Hecht, Charles Brownold, Nathan H. Hirshberg, Charles G. Hutzler, and Bernard Behrens.

Mrs. Stanford Z. (Marie) Rothschild, writing in a 1969 memoir, explained why she thought the German Jews had started their own debutante balls: "When the old Baltimore German Jewish community established some status, they must have thought it time to have formal status socially. Not being eligible for the non-Jewish Junior Assembly, they decided to have a similar setup of 'important Jewish families.'" Mrs. Rothschild felt strongly that at least in one instance, the *Sun*, in its reporting of the Harmony Ball debutantes, went out of its way to call attention to the debutantes' being Jewish. She wrote, "The morning after my debut, the *Sun* story read 'These Eight Hebrew Maidens Made Their Bow to Society Last Night.' No publicity was given to the *Sun* for a long time after *that*."

Introduced at the 1924 Harmony Ball were debutantes Miss Beatrice Engel, Miss Elsa Wolf, and Miss Elizabeth Lowenstein. In 1925, Nannette Fransdorf, Grace Deiches, Ruth Henrietta Hutzler, Louise Strouse, Doris Heineman, and Marjorie Weil bowed to society. In 1926, Isabella Strouse Fuld and Elizabeth Rosen; in 1927, Carolyn Fuld, Adelaide Rose Block, Frances Berwanger, and Bernice Simon. Mrs. Dorothy Jandorf Cohnen recalled her coming-out party in the 1930s. "It was at the Belvedere and my escort was Harry Isaacs. I still remember what I was wearing. The top of my gown was white lame, and from the waist down was white tulle, and I wore an orchid corsage. Others who were there were Phil Katz, Sam Strouse, Jay Nusbaum, Janet Wolf, and Shirley Miller. Shirley, I remember, gave a big dinner party before the ball itself. They were lovely affairs, and everything about them—what people were wearing, the flowers, the music, and especially the people. All of it seemed so important to us at least at the time."

The last year stories about the Harmony Balls appeared in the *Sun* was 1936. But Eleanor "EeeBee" Hirsh recalled that Harmony Balls continued at the Phoenix Club on Eutaw Place until 1941.

There were several reasons why the tradition of the German Jews' debutante ball came to an end. First there was the Depression: a growing poverty throughout the country had the effect of making the Harmony Balls in Baltimore, with such wealth on conspicuous display, appear both tasteless and impolitic. Second, news of what would be known as the Holocaust was reaching the country, and German refugees from that nightmare were coming to Baltimore. The mood of many German Jews in Baltimore quietly shifted; they began to focus their considerable energies first on helping Jewish refugees get to America and then on helping to support them when they got here. Much effort that had gone into creating a "Society" was now going into saving one—this one with a lowercase "s."

Still another reason the balls were discontinued: the Jews of Eastern European descent had begun to make their mark economically and were taking their places in community activities. The social and economic status that the German Jews had enjoyed over the Eastern European Jews was slowly melting away; differences in wealth and influence between the two groups were disappearing. And lastly, World War II made displays of extravagance on the home front inappropriate.

The privileged few who "came out" and danced at the Harmony Circle Balls lived in a gilded dream world of status that had been denied to them by gentiles. To those who remember that world fondly, it remains an elegant cameo in the history of Jewish Baltimore.

Lake Drive: The First "German-Russian" Neighborhood

Together, German and Russian Jews created a neighborhood that would come to be known as "Lake Drive."

In Baltimore, from the 1870s through the 1930s, the locus of German Jewish lifestyle was Eutaw Place. Moving there was an ambition realized by German Jewish families who had the wherewithal, but not all German Jews could manage it. Beginning in the 1890s, a population of German Jews with perhaps more "family" than money moved to what was for them the next best neighborhood: the streets adjoining Eutaw Place. Here they created a Jewish neighborhood that would come to be known loosely as "Lake Drive."

They were joined by the wealthier Russian Jews moving out of East Baltimore to the Lake Drive neighborhoods of Brooks Lane, Callow Avenue, Chauncey Avenue, Linden Avenue, Whitelock Street, and Brookfield Avenue. Lucille Karr, who was born and raised in the Linden-Ducatel area, remembers: "By the mid-1930s most of the neighborhood was Jewish."

Contiguous to that neighborhood and a sort of extension of it were the Auchentoroly Terrace neighborhoods, bordering Druid Hill Park and comprising Bryant Avenue, Whittier Avenue, Orem Avenue, Ruskin Avenue, and Auchentoroly Terrace itself. These streets made up their own neighborhood, alongside but hardly a part of the more elegant Eutaw Place community. In the early 1920s the Orthodox Shaarei Tfiloh Synagogue was founded at Auchentoroly Terrace, Liberty Heights Avenue, and Holmes Avenue. It is still there, functioning as a synagogue today.

Morton Gilden recalled nearby Reservoir Hill as "a well-defined neighborhood. We had Druid Hill Park on the east and the north. South of us was the high-society neighborhood of Bolton Hill. On the west was Madison Avenue, where the black neighborhood began. In that space between was a solid enclave of upwardly mobile Jews."

Kalman "Buzzy" Hettleman lived at 2503 Linden Avenue. Mr. Hettleman recalls,

> We lived across from the Weisgals, who lived at 831 Chauncey, and between the Salganiks and the Davidsons. As kids growing up in the Lake Drive neighborhood we used to play softball on the empty lot at the corner of Linden and Brooks Lane. We learned to play tennis on the courts over in Druid Hill Park.
>
> By "we," I mean David Schimmel, Benson Offit, Marty Greenfeld, Zelig Robinson, Irwin Epstein, Carole Beerman Ellin—to name a few.
>
> We all went to school P.S. 61 at Linden Avenue right above North Avenue. Across the street from the school was our favorite candy

This magnificent building at Eutaw Place and Lanvale Street was the home of the Oheb Shalom congregation from 1893 to 1960. Although Reform in its practice today, Oheb Shalom was founded in 1853 as a "middle-of-the-road" congregation, between the Reform ritual of Har Sinai and the Orthodoxy of Baltimore Hebrew.

store, Schwartzie's. A couple of houses down the block from Schwartzie's was the Communist cell where Whittaker Chambers supposedly met with his colleagues.

The prominent Jewish industrialists Jacob Epstein and L. Manuel Hendler each had a mansion on the opposite corners of Eutaw Place at Lake Drive. The most prestigious apartment house addresses in those days were the five grand buildings in the Lake Drive area—the Emersonian, Temple Gardens, the Esplanade, the Marlborough, and the Riviera.

People who grew up in these neighborhoods have put into the mythology of Jewish life in Baltimore the legendary drugstore and neighborhood rite of passage known as Manheimer's Pharmacy. Sigmund "Siggy" Shapiro, who grew up in the Eutaw Place–Lake Drive neighborhood, was a "regular" at Manheimer's up into the 1950s. He recalls,

The store had two entrances, the main one on Eutaw Place and the back entrance off the alley behind Cloverdale Road. The back entrance connected to the Emersonian.

The proprietors were Edith and Raymond Manheimer. They were childless; neither liked kids very much, particularly us kids who frequented the place. We gave them plenty of reason.

As you entered from Eutaw Place, you saw on your right two pinball machines in front of a magazine rack. Beyond was a long fountain against a wall, manned by Lettie. She was extremely dexterous with the Coke plunger, waffle iron, and seltzer spritzer.

On the back wall was a mini-kitchen, serving hot and cold food, and to the left of that was the pharmacy. The tables were in the middle of the floor. The basement housed a small bakery, which turned out, somehow, the best coconut and chocolate cake in the world.

As kids we were in and out of the place all day, and we became masters of the pinball machines—which paid off only in free games. Bobby Hess could handle a pinball machine like a brain surgeon—tickling it to within a tilt of its life. Cantor Abba Weisgal was another pinball machine player. After Shabbos he would go home, pick up his cane and make his appearance in Manheimer's. His ritual was to hang the cane on the rack, and then very seriously engage the machine in struggle. When the machine tilted on him, he would curse it in Yiddish.

The German Jewish Reform synagogues followed their congregants to Eutaw Place—Oheb Shalom moved in 1893 from South Hanover Street (between Pratt and Lombard) to Eutaw Place and Lanvale; Baltimore Hebrew relocated in 1891 from Lloyd and Watson Streets to Madison Avenue and Robert Street; and Har Sinai followed in 1894 from West Lexington Street between Pearl and Pine Streets to Bolton and Wilson Streets. In 1922, the Chizuk Amuno moved to Eutaw Place and Chauncey Avenue from McCulloh and Mosher Streets, where it had moved in 1895 from Lloyd and Lombard Streets. The building at Eutaw Place and Chauncey is now the home of the Beth Am Synagogue. Founded in 1974 as "Dr. (Louis) Kaplan's shul," the synagogue is a storehouse of memories for many who once lived in the Eutaw Place–Lake Drive neighborhood.

The Lake Drive neighborhoods, along with Mt. Washington, have a place in Baltimore Jewish history as the first and earliest venues where German Jews and Russian Jews began to live in the same neighborhoods, a trend that would accelerate over the next fifty years.

Baltimore's Second Wave of German Jews: Sponsorship Was the Key

"Sponsorship" often determined who would live and who would die.

On the night of January 1, 1930, Nazi storm troopers, driven to madness and brutality by a national culture of anti-Semitism, killed eight Jews in Berlin rioting. These martyrs were among the first Jewish victims in the early days of the Nazi reign of terror that led to the Holocaust.

When news of these atrocities traveled through Germany, Ingeborg Cohn was ten years old and living in a suburb near Leipzig. Ralph Brunn was six and living in Wertheim. Lore Wolf was seven, and her sister Ruth was three; they were living in Aachen. Before the decade was over, thousands of Jews would leave their homes in Germany and find their way to Palestine, South America, or the United States.

But chance would bring these particular children, among hundreds of others from similar circumstances, to Baltimore. The saga of how each managed to get out of Germany to the United States at the port of Baltimore and, in time, become part of Baltimore's Jewish community, is a story of uncommon fortitude, Jewish organizational genius, communal commitment, money, and luck.

Peel back layers of the process—a Jewish family's anguished decision to leave the Germany they had called home; the sad farewell to the life they had known; immigration, the long voyage; starting life over in the States— peel back the layers and you find that each journey started with a single letter of correspondence. The subject of each letter, no matter on which side of the Atlantic it originated, was the one word that could make or doom a life: "sponsorship."

Ingeborg Cohn lived with her mother and father (Charlotte and Ludwig), four sisters, and two brothers in a well-furnished three-room apartment in a comfortable suburb outside of Leipzig. The family enjoyed a particular status because Dr. Cohn was a practicing physician who was widely known and respected in the community. But the virulent anti-Semitism in Berlin found its way to Leipzig and into the lives of the Cohns. The storm troopers enforced a boycott against doing business with Jews, and Dr. Cohn soon lost most of his patients. Ingeborg and her siblings were barred from membership in the local athletic clubs; they were not allowed into the universities.

By late 1939 the family had had enough; it was time to leave. Ingeborg was nineteen.

Miss Cohn, who today is Mrs. Hans Weinberger, recalls:

To get out of Germany in those days was very, very difficult. You had to get papers and you had to turn over everything you owned—silver, jewelry, money. You could take with you maybe four hundred dollars, and you had to have a sponsor, someone who would vouch for you in writing that the person arriving in your charge would not be a burden to the government of the country.

I had a sister who had earlier emigrated to Bolivia, and so to begin, we booked passage to Bolivia, on the Chilean ship *Copiago*. But in one of those quirks of fate, the ship went first to Baltimore, where it was scheduled to pick up freight. When I heard that, I got a cable off to my boyfriend, Hans Weinberger, in Richmond, and asked him to meet me in Baltimore. He was allowed aboard ship, but I was not allowed off, so we decided to get married aboard ship.

Flora Dashew and Mrs. Simon Sobeloff of the Baltimore chapter of the National Council of Jewish Women were at the dock to meet the ship, and to provide any service to the refugees they might need. We asked them to get the waiting time of forty eight hours waived, and get a rabbi to marry us. They did both. Rabbi Abraham Shaw came aboard and married us, but only after Mrs. Sobeloff got Judge Sobeloff to waive the forty-eight-hour waiting time. I had to go on to Bolivia, but in the meantime my husband wrote a letter to the Dashews, who had already been so kind to us, and asked if they would be our sponsors. They said they would. I made it back to Baltimore shortly afterward, where my husband was waiting for me.

The Dashew family were like our own family. Mr. Dashew (Jay) gave Hans a job with his company, and the Dashew family made the Weinbergers a part of their family life.

In 1935, Ralph Brunn's father, Gustav, was living with his family in Wertheim. Shortly thereafter, the family moved to Frankfurt. In 1938, in an atmosphere of threat and discomfort, they felt it was time to leave Germany. Mr. Gustav Brunn wrote to his Uncle Abraham Baumblatt in Baltimore, who had come over from Germany after World War I.

"Uncle Abraham was very kind and offered to sponsor us," Ralph Brunn recalls. "But all was not that smooth. At about that same time my father was arrested and sent to Buchenwald. The Germans were, fortunately for us, very corruptible. And ten thousand marks, a lot of money at the time, secured his freedom. We came over to Baltimore on the North German Lloyd-Hamburg American Lines."

Another view of Eutaw Place, close to the institutions that served the German Jewish community—the Phoenix Club and Temple Oheb Shalom, Sondheim Funeral Home, Baltimore Hebrew's Madison Avenue Temple, and Har Sinai Temple, which marked the corner of Bolton and Wilson Streets, two blocks east of Eutaw Place. Chizuk Amuno (then Orthodox) stood at McCulloh and Mosher Streets; Shearith Israel (German Orthodox) was located at 2105 McCulloh Street. (Courtesy of the Peale Museum/Maryland Historical Society.)

It was because of this popular shipping line, which operated from Hamburg to Baltimore, that so many Jews emigrating from Germany in those years settled in Baltimore. Ralph Brunn, at age fourteen in 1938, was one of them.

Lore (Levi) and Ruth (Rehfeld) Wolf were ten and six, respectively, and living in Aachen in the early 1930s. When it was becoming apparent to their father that they must leave Germany, Lore recalls, "He wrote a letter to Julia Friedenwald Strauss, a woman in the States who, he had heard, was helping German Jews locate friends and relatives who might be sponsors in Baltimore.

"Events moved in such a way that Strauss—that's Julia—led to Strouse, and that's Beatrice, and to sponsorship of me by Mrs. Samuel Strouse and of Ruth by Mrs. Meyer Salabes."

The Baltimore Jewish community was quick to set up an infrastructure of support for the newcomers, beginning at the dock. Most every problem was anticipated, and sophisticated efforts were made to provide homes, apartments, furniture, medical care, schooling, jobs, synagogue affiliation, and summer camp. Samuel and Beatrice Strouse even held Sunday afternoon concerts in their Mt. Washington home. The National Council of Jewish Women offered its fairly inclusive "services for the foreign born"; Hebrew Free Loan arranged attractive loans for start-up businesses; the Associated Jewish Charities and Welfare Fund provided services to meet the spectrum of needs. The process ran smoothly under the leadership of activists in the Baltimore Jewish community—Mrs. Isaac Hamburger, Mrs. Samuel Strouse, Mrs. Henry Frank—to name only some.

That was more than fifty years ago. Those children who stood on the decks holding their parents' hands as the storied landscape of America came into view are now in their seventies and eighties. Altogether they made up a population in Baltimore of perhaps no more than a thousand (not all who came to Baltimore stayed), and many became successful professionals, businesspeople, and civic activists. They were able to get their feet quite comfortably set on the rungs of the ladder of the American dream.

In the end, they have in common their gratitude to a family member who made it all happen by writing a letter entreating for sponsorship; and to the sponsors themselves, who took the risk of sponsorship—and won.

Druid Hill Park: A "Jewish Neighborhood"

The park became an extension of the Jewish neighborhoods of Northwest Baltimore.

From the 1920s through the 1950s, almost all the neighborhoods bordering on Druid Hill Park or within walking distance of it—Lake Drive, Mondawmin, Auchentoroly Terrace, the Park Heights Avenue and Reisterstown Road neighborhoods from Fulton Avenue all the way to Pimlico—almost all of those neighborhoods were Jewish. They owed much of their character and their culture to their proximity to Druid Hill Park. The park in that era was an ongoing Jewish festival, particularly on the High Holy Days. Taking a walk in the park was what so many from the nearby neighborhoods did in the sunshine of those long-ago Rosh Hashanah afternoons.

In December 1925, a sixteen-year-old boy received a medal from the *Evening Sun* for being the best tennis player in the Baltimore Interpark Tennis Association. He went on to greater glory, playing on such famous courts as Forest Hills and competing against such greats as 1920s U.S. Open champ Bill Tilden. He then went on to win the coveted Aaron Straus Trophy at the Suburban Club.

His name was Eddie Jacobs, and in time he would become the tenth-ranked player in the United States. But young Eddie Jacobs did not come off the courts of Baltimore's country clubs, as one might have expected. He was a product of the Druid Hill Park public courts, competing with peers from the nearby neighborhoods.

Mr. Jacobs had been one of many Jewish boys and girls who belonged to the tennis club at Druid Hill Park. The alumni include Bill Jacobs (Eddie's brother), the five Thaler brothers (George, Tim, Larry, Bill, and Joe), Adrienne Goldberg Hoffman (among the highest ranked women players of her time), Kalman "Buzzy" Hettleman (who ranked among the top fifty players in the country and won the city championship eight times), Dave Freishtat, Malcolm Fox, and Dave Schimmel.

According to Mr. Hettleman, training at the Druid Hill Park courts was tough. "We started when we were as young as nine and ten. We lived just across the way on the streets by the lake, so we would walk over easily," he recalls. "It didn't matter how hot it was, we played. If it snowed, our instructor, Maury Schwartzman, had us shovel off the courts. In the cold, we played with gloves."

"By the way," Mr. Hettleman continues, "I played Arthur Ashe on the Druid Hill Park courts. I beat him, too. But he was twelve and I was twenty."

On Sunday mornings, the neighborhood's young people would rent bikes from Mr. Davis's Cycle Shop, on Park Circle at its junction with Park Heights Avenue and Druid Park Drive. By ten o'clock on any fine sunny Sunday morning, all of Mr. Davis's bicycles were rented out, including his only "bicycle built for two." The cyclers rode every path of the park, down to what is now the Reptile House, past the Zoo, up to what teenagers knew as "Prospect Hill," and as far as the tennis courts and swimming pool.

The "Mansion House" was known to the Jewish children of the 1930s as a peanut and hot dog concession. But in the summer of 1938, this aged mansion, close to the Zoo, opened as a first-class restaurant, advertising extravagantly: "Leisurely dining on broad porches under gaily colored umbrellas lighted at night by huge lanterns that cast a romantic glow." Diners were invited to climb up into the observation tower, which commanded a clear view of the city, and to listen to string music out on the porch with the undulated green slopes of Druid Hill Park as a backdrop. But the restaurant had a problem from the day it opened; it could not get a liquor license because Maryland would not make an exception to the law prohibiting the sale of alcohol in parks. The Mansion House restaurant closed after three years.

The Druid Hill Park boat lake, now the waterfowl conservatory, was frozen solid in the coldest times of the winter, and the park service kept the surface well hosed so that the lake froze evenly for skaters' pleasure. There was an island in the middle of the lake that served as a refuge where one could huddle close to the fires that skaters kept going to ward off the evening's chill. There was no canned music, no orderly counter-clockwise traffic pattern; skaters glided this way and that, following their hearts' desires. There was only the sound of slashing blades breaking the silence under the cold stars.

Windsor Hills: Notable Families in a Historic Time and Place

It was a unique neighborhood in the history of Jewish Baltimore.

Strictly speaking, Windsor Hills from the turn of the twentieth century through the 1950s was not considered a Jewish neighborhood, an assessment with which its resident Jewish families would agree. A glance at the city directories of those years shows that non-Jews there probably did make up a modest majority.

But for Baltimore's Jewish population, the Windsor Hills community had a special character about it. Many of the families who lived there were descendants of the established Jewish families, mostly German, a few of Eastern European origin. Some of the families traced their beginnings in Baltimore as far back as the mid-nineteenth century. It was the concentration of these families, with their community prominence, family lineage, and wealth, that gave Windsor Hills its unique place in local Jewish history.

The Joseph Ulmans lived at 2615 Talbot Road. When Judge Ulman died, the *Sunpapers* referred to him as a "jurist of national reputation." A graduate of the Johns Hopkins University and Columbia School of Law, he was appointed judge of the Supreme Bench by Governor Albert C. Ritchie in 1924 while a partner in the firm of Knapp, Ulman, and Tucker. In his long career of public service, Judge Ulman served as president of the Hebrew Benevolent Society and vice president of the Baltimore Chapter of the American Jewish Congress. The Joseph Ulmans are said to have been the first Jewish family to move into Windsor Hills, in the year 1910. The Hutzler and Hollander families soon followed.

The Shakman Katzes lived at 2609 Talbot Road. Mr. Katz was the proprietor of K. Katz men's clothiers, located at 7 to 9 East Baltimore Street, and was married to the former Amalie Sonneborn, the daughter of Siegmund and Camille Sonneborn. Siegmund was a member of Henry Sonneborn and Company, which in its glory days of the early twentieth century was one of the largest manufacturers of men's suits in the world.

John Z. Katz, son of Shakman and Amalie Katz, grew up in the family home in Windsor Hills. With friends from the neighborhood, he went to Park School (where both his father and mother had graduated) and then to Haverford College. He recalls, "First Park School, then Haverford—that was the Windsor Hills pattern. There seemed to be another pattern to growing up in Windsor Hills, at least for the boys. To meet a lot of girls, we traveled over to the Park Heights area. I remember Margot Hess, Patsy Miller, Anne Weiler."

The Sidney Berneys lived at 2605 Talbot Road. Berney-Hamburger family history includes names that resonate through the community: Isaac and Betty Hamburger, Albert Hutzler, Gretchen Hochschild Hutzler, and Alice and Jerold Hoffberger. Sidney Berney and brother Albert were descendants of Isaac Hamburger, founder of the popular clothing store at Baltimore and Hanover Streets, which Albert eventually headed. In his time, Albert became a leader in the Baltimore Jewish community and local civic life. A bachelor when he died in 1940, at age sixty-two, he was survived by brothers Bertram, Joseph, and Sidney (another brother, Louis, had died only two months earlier), and a sister Fannie, mother of Walter Sondheim, Jr.

The Walter Sondheim, Jr., family lived at 4006 Alto Road, among other Windsor Hills addresses. Mr. Sondheim was an executive with Hochschild, Kohn, and Company for many years and became a leader in Baltimore's mercantile and civic life. "That's the house where my sister Ellie Dankert and I grew up," said his son, John.

The Rothschild family, ca. 1890. *Left to right*, Solomon Rothschild, Hanna Rothschild (nee Lowenberg, Sol's first wife), Moses Rothschild, Mollie Florsheim (a Rothschild by birth), Carrie Feldenheimer (also Rothschild by birth), and Aaron Rothschild. The brothers Solomon and Moses Rothschild came to Baltimore in 1875 from Bavaria. Fifteen years later they formed an insurance company, the Immediate Sick Benefit Society, which in time would become Sun Life Insurance Company of America. The company grew to be among the largest life insurance companies in America. The Rothschilds sold their interest in the company in 1971. (Courtesy of Stanford Rothschild.)

The Paul Wolman family, including well-known sons Benjamin and Paul Jr., lived at 2701 Lawina Road. Jeanette Wolman recalled her house-hunting days: "My husband, Paul, and I looked everywhere," she says. "We liked Forest Park and Mt. Washington and Park Heights, but we fell in love with Windsor Hills." Mrs. Wolman, born and raised in New York, had completed two years of Goucher College before entering the University of Maryland School of Law. She graduated in the school's second class ever to include women, and she was the first woman admitted to the Baltimore bar.

The Alan and Manfred Guttmacher families were longtime residents of Windsor Hills, residing at 2700 Lawina Road and 2704 Queen Anne Road, respectively. Sons of Rabbi Adolf Guttmacher of the Baltimore Hebrew Congregation, the Guttmacher brothers were identical twins who distinguished themselves in medicine. Manfred, who died in 1966, gained international fame for his work in forensic psychiatry; Alan was a high-profile champion of birth control.

Other prominent families living in Windsor Hills included the Jacob Blausteins (who founded American Oil), the Henry Rosenbergs (Crown Central Petroleum), and Bryllion Fagin, renowned author and professor of drama at Johns Hopkins, who founded Theater Hopkins. Edward, Walter, and Jerome Swartz, three brothers who lived within a block of one another, operated the Swartz men's clothing discount house, whose national reputation rested on its clientele of Washington politicians. Other neighbors included Louis H. Levin, who was married to Rabbi Benjamin Szold's daughter, Bertha, and was a distinguished Jewish activist in Baltimore from the turn of the century to the 1920s. His contributions to Jewish communal life were so revered that Levindale Hebrew Home and Hospital was named in his honor. Jacob Beser was a member of the crew of the *Enola Gay* when that airplane dropped the first atomic bomb on Hiroshima. Famed writer William Styron (*Sophie's Choice*) spent many hours writing at the Lawina Road home of his mother-in-law, Selma Burgunder. No fewer than four generations of Hollanders made their home in Windsor Hills.

This small aristocracy of Jewish families, who shared community involvement, family standing, wealth, and a Windsor Hills address, created a unique chapter in local Jewish history. In years to come, the Windsor Hills of around 1900 through the 1950s will be seen as a historic time and place in which notable Jewish families in the arts, academia, the professions, civic affairs, and communal life came together in a leafy neighborhood hugging the slopes of Gwynns Falls Park in the western reaches of Baltimore City.

Mt. Washington: Next Stop, North and West, for Baltimore's German Jews

The community was ideal— neither "restricted" nor "too Jewish."

In a time frame roughly spanning the years from 1830 to 1900, the same years in which the German Jews first settled in East Baltimore and began their move to Eutaw Place and Lake Drive, another neighborhood was forming in Baltimore County that would play a part in the history of Jewish Baltimore, Mt. Washington.

In 1850, real estate entrepreneur George Gelbach had an interesting idea: a person could work in the city and live in the "country," a relatively new concept for Baltimore. Most small-business owners lived and worked in the same city neighborhood, often in the same house "over the store." But Mt. Washington would be different. It would be a summer colony, offering Baltimoreans a "commuter neighborhood."

The public bought the idea. Mt. Washington in the 1890s and early twentieth century became a sylvan village far from the city, linked by the railroad that ran up the Jones Falls Valley (sometimes called the "Ruxton Rocket"). Many of the wealthy Jewish people living in town during the winter chose to buy summer vacation homes in Mt. Washington, and some of them who started as summer vacation homeowners wound up living there the year round.

Among the families with summer homes in Mt. Washington, Jewish and non-Jewish, was that of H. L. Mencken. The Mencken family home was high on a ridge on Belvedere Avenue, overlooking what is now the south side of Northern Parkway. A young Henry Mencken spent his boyhood summers there.

For the German Jews moving out of Eutaw Place and Lake Drive, Mt. Washington had a certain tone. It was leafy, with lovely traditional brick and clapboard houses along winding, tree-lined streets that were more like country roads. It had a lacrosse club, a clubhouse, an improvement association, and several social clubs. And most significantly, Mt. Washington was never restricted, in spirit or in letter. There is no record of ads or signs that read "No Jews Allowed" in Mt. Washington.

All of this made Mt. Washington an ideal neighborhood for German Jews who wanted to move out of Eutaw Place and Lake Drive but not into the Park Heights corridor, which some undoubtedly felt to be "too Jewish." In the first three decades of the twentieth century, Mt. Washington, once largely Protestant and Catholic, would become a mix of Catholic, Protestant, and Jewish. By the 1930s, much of the German Jewish population that had been living on Eutaw Place and Lake Drive had moved to Mt. Washington.

At the same time, change caught up with the Phoenix Club, whose membership began to lose its German Jewish cast. Russian Jews who could afford it replaced German Jews who could not and who resigned for a variety of reasons. After World War II, the community's flight out of the city continued, and in those leafier settings Jewish Baltimore found the same social amenities in the Suburban Club (founded in 1901), plus golf and swimming. The Phoenix Club membership dwindled. The club finally disbanded in 1959 and sold its property to the Amalgamated Clothing Workers of America. The organization tore down the building and erected one of its own.

There is no "Jewish Society" today—not of the kind defined by members of the Phoenix Club and of the Suburban Club in earlier days. Exclusivity may not have disappeared entirely, but the two strands of Jewish social life, German and Russian, have been drawn together (philanthropy has replaced ancestry as the tie that binds). Many young people in both the Jewish and gentile communities have rejected the social caste system of their elders as irrelevant. To many of them, one's family wealth, or standing, or country of origin matters much less than it once did, or matters not at all.

Henrietta Szold was born in Baltimore on South Eutaw Street, daughter of Rabbi Benjamin Szold of the Oheb Shalom congregation and Sophia Schaar Szold. Though of Central European background, she was drawn to help East Baltimore's Russian Jewish immigrants. She was loved and respected for creating the "Russian Night School" there. From Baltimore to New York and Palestine, she became actively involved in Zionism, Hadassah, and Youth Aliyah.

Facing page: The 1906 Confirmation Class of Temple Oheb Shalom, a photograph in the possession of Jacob Blaustein's daughter, Barbara Blaustein Hirschhorn. First row, *left to right:* Jacob Blaustein (then sixteen and living at 2316 Callow Avenue, he went on to become a leading industrialist, philanthropist, and public servant), Justine Kell, Rabbi William Rosenau, Rosalind Carroll, Walter Mayer, Albert H. Samuel. Top Row, *left to right,* Miriam G. Klein, Estelle S. Stern, Hilda Katz (who would become Mrs. Jacob Blaustein), Florette Hamburger, Veronica Oppenheim, Teresa Cohen. The students lived within walking distance of the temple—on Newington Avenue, Linden Avenue, Madison Avenue, and Whitelock Street. (Courtesy of Barbara Blaustein Hirschhorn.)

The Katzensteins, ca. 1910. *Left to right;* Edgar, Carrie, Benjamin, Fannie, Herbert, Louis, William, Milton, and Birdie. All nine were the children of Abraham and Matilda Schwartz Katzenstein. According to family history, Matilda's parents immigrated from the German province of Wurttemburg, near the Black Forest, in the early 1840s; the origins of Abraham's family, also thought to be in one of the German provinces, are less certain. Benjamin and William Katzenstein ("B. Katzenstein and Brother") manufactured men's and women's overcoats and topcoats at 107 West Fayette Street. (Courtesy of the Katzenstein family.)

Above: "Little Joe" Wiesenfeld out for a trot with horse and carriage on Lake Drive in 1910. Afternoon carriage rides through Druid Hill Park were popular with the Eutaw Place gentry. With this matched pair of horses, Wiesenfeld won a blue ribbon in a New York horse show—a feat considered at the time to be unusual for a Jew and especially so for a Jew from Baltimore.

Right: Joel Hutzler at age twenty, in U.S. Navy uniform. Born to David Hutzler and Ella Gutman (of the Julius Gutman department store family), Joel graduated from Friends School in 1911 and from Johns Hopkins University in 1915. He worked for a short time at a department store in Newark, New Jersey, before joining the family business. When war intervened, he attended officer's school and entered the Navy as an ensign. Later he was active in civic and Jewish service—as treasurer of both the YM and YWHA and director of the Associated Guidance Bureau.

The Hendler family, ca. 1925: In the back, on chairs, are (*left*) "Bubba" Sophia Duke, mother of Rose D. Hendler, and (*right*) "Bubba" Belle Hendler, mother of L. Manuel Hendler. In the second row (*left to right*) are Albert "Buddy" Hendler, son of L. Manuel and Rose; Fannie Levenson, sister of Rose D. Hendler; Leonard Levenson, son of Fannie Levenson; Bernice Hendler, daughter of L. Manuel and Rose; and Ben (Bernard) Hendler, brother of L. Manuel Hendler. In the front (*left to right*) are youngsters Naomi "Pudgy" Hendler, daughter of L. Manuel and Rose, and Naomi Levin, niece of L. Manuel and Rose; Florence "Tootsie" Hendler, daughter of L. Manuel and Rose; L. Manuel Hendler; and his wife, Rose D. Hendler.

Right: This picture of Miss Jane Strouse (Kahn) appeared in a *Sun* story about a Harmony Circle debutante ball headlined, "These Eight Hebrew Maidens Made Their Bow to Society Last Night." Mrs. Stanford (Marie) Rothschild, in a 1969 memoir of the occasion, and sensitive to the Jewish debutantes being singled out in the paper as "Hebrew Maidens," commented, "No publicity was given to the *Sun* for a long time after *that*!"

Below: The Hollander children on the steps of their home at 2513 Talbot Road in 1916. *Left to right:* Edward at six years old; Sidney at six months; Edith at four years. Four generations of Hollanders made their home in Windsor Hills.

Doing Business

Hutzler's: The Family and the Family Store

The first meeting to organize Har Sinai congregation was held in Moses Hutzler's home.

On a Saturday morning in the late 1940s, two teenage girls made plans to meet downtown. The destination was no more specific than that, just "downtown," but neither had a moment of uncertainty about where they would catch up with each other: both headed for "Hutzler's Balcony." Of course. Through the late 1960s, Hutzler's Balcony, off of the department store's Saratoga Street entrance between Eutaw and Howard Streets, was the great Saturday morning meeting place for women of all ages shopping downtown.

"You met all of your friends there, all you had to do was show up," recalls Bette Davis Cohen:

It was a long and narrow area, and always crowded with people meeting people. As you entered, there was, off to your left, a bakery counter, and off to your right a long, wide counter for checking packages and coats. And on that counter, the most popular attraction of the whole balcony an open notebook.

Friends wrote notes to each other in the notebook, transforming it into a virtual message center for a certain group of downtown shoppers. You could always run through the messages and check out who was downtown, and where they were going to be and what they planned to do. It was a wonderful system.

To Baltimore girls coming of age, from the 1930s through the 1960s, Hutzler's was indispensable. With its excellent service and its prestigious

By the time George W. Howard published his 1873 volume in praise of Baltimore, *The Monumental City, Its Past History and Present Resources,* in which this image appeared, Joel Gutman already had established himself on North Eutaw Street as a leading wholesaler and retailer of fine clothing and accessories. The firm flourished well into the twentieth century.

lines, Hutzler's was the closest Baltimoreans got to haute couture. Shopping, meeting friends, having lunch, and even returning things to Hutzler's were experiences that became part of the teenage rite of passage.

The balcony as meeting place was pure Hutzler's, providing a depth of inventive personal service that bonded customer to institution in a way that—many of the store's alumni employees and customers feel—has never been duplicated, before or since.

On a summer afternoon in the early 1940s, a teenage Joan Strouse sat on her front steps in Mt. Washington when a friend happened by. In the course of their conversation, Joan mentioned that she was waiting for a package due momentarily on the Hutzler delivery truck. "I bought it yesterday," she said. The comment created no surprise. Next day or even same-day delivery, no matter how large or small the purchase, was part of Hutzler's policy of "charge and send." Hutzler's policy held that "anything could be returned within a reasonable amount of time," leaving the definition of "reasonable" wide open. It was said that many people returned items to Hutzler's they'd bought at Stewart's or Hochschild's.

Miss Strouse (who became Mrs. Gilbert Sandler) remembers: "The delivery policy was such that you could call Hutzler's for spools of thread or handkerchiefs or tubes of lipstick in the morning and have it all delivered early that afternoon. Delivery was free. If you changed your mind about the color of something, for example, a maroon Hutzler truck would pick up the item later that afternoon and have your second choice color to you no later than the following morning."

Daniel Sachs worked for Hutzler's downtown store, with a few short interruptions, from 1957 to 1981, and recalls them as the "twenty-four happiest years" of his life. "I used to see people, mostly older women, come to Hutzler's in the morning and stay there all day!" he says. "They'd shop department by department, relax in our sixth floor lounge, then eat in one of the restaurants, the Colonial, the Fountain Shop, the Luncheonette in the Budget Store or the Quixie Shop on the sixth floor, and then shop the rest of the afternoon until closing. Hutzler's was that kind of a store."

Shirley Broad Kaufman has vivid memories of the Quixie Shop. "It was quick," she says, "in the sense that service was fast. But it was operated on an unusual concept. The help was drawn from Baltimore's mentally retarded population, and the operation was geared to their ability."

Mr. Sachs held a number of positions in the Hutzler's management, including buyer in the toy department and later in men's sportswear. "Our toy department carried everything. Metal trucks, Tonka Toys, electric trains, Erector sets, board games like Monopoly, and all kinds of battery-operated toys," he says. "We introduced the Barbie dolls to Baltimore, and also a popular doll named Chatty Cathy. You pulled her string and she would talk."

In addition, Mr. Sachs recalls, "Hutzler's had a camera department, a Boy Scout department, record department, sporting goods department, book department. We had it all! The largest department was always the women's and men's clothing. We had only the class brands like McGregor, Puritan, Robert Bruce, Hathaway, London Fog. But in time the discount stores came to town, and we could not compete." Reflecting on his years of service, Mr. Sachs says Hutzler's was a "class act." "The family treated us as part of their own family, and as employees we were often invited to Albert Hutzler's Pomona estate, where the Pikesville Hilton is today."

Moses Hutzler, according to Hutzler family history, emigrated to the United States in 1838 from the Bavarian town of Hagenbach. In time, he opened a little store on Baltimore's Eutaw Street, became the father of Hutzler brothers Abram, David, and Charles, and, prospering, moved the store to Howard and Clay Streets.

The Baltimore circle in which the family flourished was distinctly German Jewish, with its Phoenix Club, Harmony Club debutante balls, Suburban Club, and Reform congregations, a society between the Protestant world and the Jewish world. To a highly visible extent, German Jews perpetuated that society by marrying into one another's families.

As early as 1842, the Hutzler family was involved in local Jewish affairs. Moses Hutzler was active in forming what came to be known as Har Sinai,

Abram G. Hutzler, ca. 1900. He, along with brothers David and Charles, were the sons of Moses Hutzler, who came to America from the Bavarian town of Hagenbach in 1838. Moses founded Hutzler's in 1858. With its liberal return policy and upscale merchandise, the store became a Baltimore legend. The family remained active in Baltimore's religious, civic, and philanthropic life.

and in 1842 the first meeting of the Reform Congregation was held at Mr. Hutzler's home at Exeter Street and Eastern Avenue. Abram Hutzler became a Bar Mitzvah in a temporary meeting place before the dedication of the Har Sinai sanctuary in 1855. And according to a historical account of Har Sinai written by the congregation's Rabbi Abraham Shusterman, Mr. Abram Hutzler provided friends and family "an interesting description of his Bar Mitzvah service as almost Orthodox, with covered heads, the separation of the sexes, and the use of a Shabbos Goy to light the fires." At Har Sinai's fiftieth anniversary celebration banquet, on November 19, 1892, David Hutzler, another son of Moses Hutzler, served as toastmaster. David Hutzler served as president of the Associated Jewish Charities and Welfare Fund from 1923 to 1925; his grandson, Albert D. Hutzler, Jr., served from 1967 to 1969.

Fame and recognition also came to Elsa Hutzler, wife of Charles G. Hutzler, II, though not from the world of commerce but from the world of art. Mrs. Hutzler was an accomplished sculptor whose work was widely exhibited here in Baltimore, in New York, and at the Corcoran Gallery in Washington, D.C. She died in 1953, at the age of forty-six.

Morton Oppenheimer, a longtime Har Sinai congregant and a student of the temple's history, observes, "It's probably true that there has been a Hutzler holding a seat in Har Sinai since Moses helped to found the place in 1842, down through David Hutzler, III, today." Yet by the 1990s, there was no local Hutzler family presence in Baltimore to compare to the family's presence here in its glory days. The business was gone from the retailing scene. Today, only a few members of the family live in Baltimore.

Is Hutzler's missed? "Ask anybody who used to shop there," said Mr. Sachs. "Thinking about what this town has lost with the closing of Hutzler's. Well, there is no store like it today. I could break down and cry."

June of 1984 brought Baltimoreans a bittersweet experience. Hutzler's was auctioning off bits and pieces of its yesterdays, and Baltimoreans were invited to come in and bid on a few artifacts that once made up the displays in the windows and around the sales floors. Hutzler's called it "the Great Attic Adventure." It was a farewell to a great lady.

Up for bids were carousel horses, glass display cases, chandeliers, wicker forms, Oriental paper parasols, jukeboxes, fishnets, tin lanterns, flags, pennants, ceiling fans, copper tree branches, and mannequins. Jane Hawkins, Hutzler's director of special events, said at the time, "Some items went for a nickel." A nickel? To own a piece of Hutzler's? To Baltimoreans that must surely have seemed like a bargain.

In the end it was the auctioneer, Jonathan Melnick, who unknowingly told the Hutzler story as well as it would ever be told. "Going. Going. Gone."

Baltimore's Retail Furniture Stores: "Closed for the Jewish Holiday"

On the Jewish High Holy Days, most of the retail furniture stores had signs on their doors, 'Closed for the Jewish Holiday.'

Certain industries in Baltimore appear to be, or historically have been, mostly under Jewish ownership. The scrap metal business is one; wholesaling and pawn brokering are others. Still another, one that in size and presence today is hardly recognizable against the memory of it, is the retail furniture business. Pollack's, Gomprecht and Benesch, Shaivitz, Little Potts, Levenson and Klein—so many of those venerable Jewish family names that were household words in Baltimore's once giant retail furniture business are now history.

It is hard to know with certainty which of the furniture stores was the oldest, but a review of their history would suggest it was Pollack's. Abraham Pollack founded the store in 1847 at 315 North Howard Street when he was nineteen. The business prospered, and not too many years later his son, Uriah, joined him. In the 1880s Pollack's was advertising "The latest and handsomest designs in Parlor Suites, Fancy Chairs and Rockers, Couches, and Room Suites in Mahogany, Oak, Walnut, and Cherry." At some point the business moved to 306 North Howard Street. Uriah Pollack died in 1897 at his home at 315 North Eutaw Street. He was a member of B'nai Brith, Har Sinai congregation, and had been a director of what is now Sinai Hospital. The store closed in 1982, by that time known as Pollack-Blum's, a part of Reliable Stores Corporation.

Gomprecht and Benesch traces its origins to 1901, when Jacob Gomprecht and Jesse Benesch opened what they called "The Store of the Largest Assortments" at 316 North Eutaw Street. It prospered from the start; the next year the store advertised that it had "the largest display of carpeting in the entire South," and in 1912 offered "delivery by auto truck." In its time it became one of Baltimore's leading upscale Jewish-owned furniture stores; it closed its doors forever on July 25, 1961. In a personal letter to his customers taken out as a full-page newspaper ad, Jesse Benesch, Jr., said goodbye to all his employees and customers.

Moses Shaivitz founded M. Shaivitz Furniture Company at 816 South Charles Street in 1891. According to his grandson Jules Shaivitz, "Moses' sons, my father Sol and my Uncle Henry, both quit school in their teens to join the family business in the early 1900s."

Isaac Hamburger and Sons store, at 122 East Baltimore Street, 1894. The company formed in 1850, when Isaac Hamburger, a twenty-year-old from Neidenburg (or Darmstadt; there are two versions), Germany, borrowed three hundred dollars to open a store at 32 Harrison Street. Hamburger actually had started in business a few years earlier in East Baltimore, as a peddler selling woolen caps that his wife made. By the turn of the century Hamburgers had stores in Washington, D.C.; Frederick, Maryland; Wilmington, Delaware; and Charlottesville and Lynchburg, Virginia. In 1906, Hamburgers opened an eight-story landmark building at Baltimore and Hanover Streets.

Hamburgers' management, 1964, *Standing, left to right:* Henry Berney, Robert Berney, Edward Hamburger. *Seated:* Betty Hamburger, Albert Berney.

Because of another similar-looking family business name in South Baltimore during that time, "Shavitz Furniture," the M. Shaivitz family identified its store by asking its customers to "Look for the clock in the middle of the block," referring to the clock that was built into the store's sign above its main entrance on Charles Street. In the pattern of Jewish family-owned furniture stores, Sol and Henry Shaivitz were succeeded into the third generation by Jules and Henry's son Bernard ("Buddy") and

Henry's son-in-law Manny Sellman. M. Shaivitz closed in 1992, one hundred and one years after Moses Shaivitz founded the business.

Little Potts was a Potts family institution at 2112 East Monument Street from 1911 to 1981. The business was founded by Isaac Potts; his son Efrem joined him in the business in 1949. Efrem recalls, "We kept the store closed for both days of Rosh Hashanah and for Yom Kippur, and for many years so did Levenson and Klein up the street."

Levenson and Klein's beginnings go back to 1919, in a corner row house at Fayette and Washington Streets. Joseph Klein, Jr., recalls:

> My father, Joseph, quit City College at fourteen to work for Max Hochschild as a runner. They had no phones and so Mr. Hochschild had my father follow him and run messages around. He left Hochschild's and opened his store at Fayette and Washington Streets. It so happened that another young man was also in the furniture business, working as credit manager for Blum's on Gay Street. His name was Reuben Levenson and he was married to my father's older sister, Miriam. The agreement was that Mr. Levenson would work in my father's store nights, and hold on to his day job at Blum's. But the business, by this time known as Levenson and Klein, prospered and so Mr. Levenson quit Blum's and came to work full time for Levenson and Klein. In 1935 the business moved to Monument and Chester Streets into the former Homin's slaughterhouse site. The business flourished through the years and with the times. Our family, the Kleins, sold to the Levenson family in 1959. After a series of sales and management changes, Levenson and Klein, which had been started by my father in 1919, finally closed its doors in 1990.

Herbert Shofer is the second generation of the Shofer family to own and operate Shofer's Furniture Company, the South Baltimore landmark that survives and still flourishes as a family institution at 930 South Charles Street. Henry "Hank" Shofer, Herb's son and grandson of founder Harry, now serves as its president. Founder Harry explained Shofer's origins this way: "In 1904, the year of the big fire, I got off the boat at Locust Point and wound up repairing bicycles. That is the story of Shofer's Furniture."

Mr. Herbert Shofer has his own view of what happened to Baltimore's retail furniture business and the many Jewish furniture stores:

> There were many forces coming together beginning in the 1960s. The

introduction of discount sales, the coming into the business of the popular priced chains like Levitz and Ikea, catalog sales, direct factory-customer operations such as Rowe, Thomasville, the collapse of downtown as a shopping area, the increasing competition for the consumer's spendable dollars. All of these problems were simply too much for many of the furniture retailers to deal with. We have been fortunate in that our market position, catering to the upscale, and our location in what turned out to be the very popular and attractive Inner Harbor, have helped make us among the survivors.

If you have any doubts that the retail furniture business in Baltimore was dominated by Jewish families, listen to this reminiscence of Jules Shaivitz. "Up until the 1950s, first day of Rosh Hashanah and Yom Kippur were not the best days to shop for furniture in Baltimore. Most of the furniture stores, being Jewish-owned, had a sign in the door, 'Closed for the Jewish Holiday.'"

S O M E, but surely not all of the Jewish family-owned furniture stores serving Baltimore in the 1950s were:

Henry Checket and Co., 412 N. Eutaw St.
Al Fradkin Co., 209 W. Fayette St.
Grand Rapids, 501 N. Howard St.
Howard Furniture, 109 N. Howard St.
Kovens Furniture Co., 1333 W. Baltimore St.
Levin Furniture, 842 W. North Ave.
Lee Furniture, 630 W. Baltimore St.
Mazer, 345 N. Charles St.
Royal, 321 W. Lombard St.

Scrap Business: Rags (and "Bones and Bottles") to Riches

In the early morning of a day in, say, 1908, a lone figure pushes a cart through the back alleys of East Baltimore. He stops to pick up discarded rags, bottles, bones, broken toys, bundles of paper, wire, shards of glass, pots and pans. He packs the items into his already-overflowing cart. What he doesn't find lying in the alley, he picks out of trash cans. All the while, his cry echoes through the dense neighborhoods: "Any rags, any bones, any bottles today?"

At the end of the day, men like him, scratching out an uncertain living at the turn of the last century, wheel their carts back to any one of a number of "junk dealers." These dealers, who bought junk cheap and sold it dear, founded the "junk yards" that would grow, some one hundred years later, into Baltimore's gargantuan scrap industry.

These men (or in some cases the men they worked for) built massive businesses, sprawling industrial complexes that gathered and converted what most would think of as junk into the stuff of megadollars, romance, and international empire. Most all of them were Jewish, recent immigrants themselves or children of immigrants, and so the scrap business in Baltimore, as it did elsewhere in America, evolved as a "Jewish business."

The "junk business" became megadollars, romance, empire.

SOME OF the prominent names in this business were (and in many cases still are) Schapiro and Shapiro, Klaff, Schloss, Plant, Lazinsky, Landsman, Hettleman, Zuckerman, Barth, Liebowitz, Kahan, Epstein, and Cohen.

In 1902, sixteen-year-old Morris Schapiro of Latvia, then part of Czarist Russia, booked passage in steerage on the S.S. *Pennsylvania*, bound for New York's Ellis Island. Twenty years later, in 1922, he would buy the S.S. *Penn*

In 1897 Max Hochschild formed a partnership with Benno and Louis Kohn, and together they opened Hochschild, Kohn, and Company, here shown on the northwest corner of Howard and Lexington Streets in this 1930 picture. Hochschild brought along his cousin, Walter Sondheim, Sr., who had worked with him in his Gay Street business (the Sondheims had immigrated from Frankfurt am Main in the mid-1860s). In time, management of the company fell to Martin Kohn, Louis B. Kohn II, Walter Sondheim, Jr., and Richard Wyman, nephew of Martin Kohn.

"Hochschild's" grew to be among the largest of Baltimore department stores. At its peak, in addition to its main store at Howard and Lexington Streets, there were five suburban outlets. In 1966 the family sold the company to out-of-town interests, and soon Mr. Sondheim, Jr., retired, assuming varied leadership roles in Baltimore civic life.

"Our First Coal Truck: C. Hoffberger and Company originally sold ice, coal, and wood, but the firm rose to prominence as a leading distributor of fuel oil. The business started out in 1892 with one horse-drawn wagon at 1108 Low Street. In 1923 the company built an ice plant at 1507 North Gay Street, and, in 1928, a cold storage facility at 530 East Monument Street. Still another expansion put company facilities at Braddish Avenue and Baker Street. In 1947 the fifth and final ice plant was built at 715 South Haven Street. According to a profile of the company in the trade journal *Industrial Power* in 1947, the "company is built around the seven Hoffberger brothers, all of whom are on the Board of Directors: Mr. Harry Hoffberger is president; Mr. Jack Hoffberger is vice president; Mr. Saul Hoffberger secretary and treasurer; the other four brothers are directors."

sylvania and junk it. But in August 1902, fresh out of the Ellis Island immigration center, he took a train to Boston, "because," he said, "that is as far as my money would take me."

Over the next two years the young Schapiro became a butcher's helper, then a grocer's clerk. All the while, he would recall in later years, life became drearier. In desperation he put together a hundred dollars and fled to Atlanta, to his only relative in America, a cousin who set him up as an itinerant peddler with a mule, a stock of soap, and a wad of dry goods. The job lasted a day. "I couldn't see pushing that stuff for a living. So with another stake, this time twelve dollars and seventy five cents, I headed for Savannah." Wandering about the seaport, he saw a sign that would shape his destiny and leave a mark forever on the city of Baltimore: "Passage to Baltimore, $12.00."

The boat that took young Morris Schapiro from Savannah docked in Baltimore in 1904, at a time when Baltimore's downtown lay flat, smoldering, and devastated from the Great Fire. The bewildered Schapiro, facing so unpromising a scene, had seventy-five cents in his pocket. He was eighteen.

By the end of 1904, young Schapiro had thirty dollars and a determination to set up his own business. Two relatives from Latvia were in Baltimore at the time; the three together put up four hundred dollars and founded the Boston Iron and Metals Company in a shed at Thames Street and Broadway. The name "Boston" was a sentimental gesture to the city where the young immigrant Morris Schapiro had spent his first night in America.

"I went into business in Baltimore," he would tell friends years later, "because that is where the boat took me. If it had taken me to Chicago I would have been in business in Chicago."

IN 1901, fifteen-year-old Harry Klaff arrived in Baltimore from Russia and found himself in an East Baltimore, as he recalled it, "of junkmen's horses' clip-clopping through the streets dragging wagons loaded with hides, skins, furs, metal, and rubber." He was working for his father, Benjamin Klaff. "I went into the scrap business with my father," he said, "because I didn't have enough money to start in anything else."

According to James Effron, who is associated with the surviving business, Keywell Corporation, the elder Klaff had been a peddler on Maryland's Eastern Shore, selling pots and pans and knives and forks door to door. A familiarity with the value of metal seemed to draw Benjamin Klaff to the scrap business, and ultimately he went into it "on a small scale." Reminiscing years after he retired, Harry Klaff told a friend, "I traveled on horseback through every state in the Union laying the groundwork for our business. Some of the horses were blue-ribbon horses. They were beauties. Then the trucks came on the scene, the business changed. It got to be mechanized."

Early on, the "B. Klaff Company" became the "H. Klaff and Company" family business. It started soon after the turn of the century with $147 in

Rear of Moses Isaac Berman's vestmaking shop at 211 North Front Street, 1893. Berman stands in the back row, holding a vest with tape measure around his neck. He and his family lived in a house next door to the shop. His brother, Solomon Berman, is in the back row, second from the right (with tie and suspenders). He had only recently arrived from Riga, Latvia, having served for three years in the Russian army, where he had learned fine hand tailoring.

cash on Central Avenue at Monument Street, where P.S. 102 (Thomas G. Hayes Elementary) stands today. Harry Klaff recalled, "It was tough sledding. We were no sooner doing business when the City of Baltimore decided to evict us and build a school on the land." In 1915, the company purchased the property at Ostend and Ridgely Streets.

SOLOMON SCHAPIRO came to Baltimore from Lemburg, Austria, in 1907. In the old country he had been a prosperous merchant selling woolen piece goods to factories all over Europe. Telling the story almost three quarters of a century later, his son Bernard recalled, "We grew up in a big home and were educated by tutors. This was the time of the Hapsburgs and I remember vividly the soldiers marching through the streets of Lemburg, their steps keeping time with the music of the marching bands." Bernard Schapiro himself was seven when he, his parents, and his ten-year-old brother Joe came here. They moved into a flat on Fayette Street. Mr. Bernard "Ben" Schapiro said, "I saw filthy gutters and outhouses, which I did not see in Lemburg."

The founding Schapiros handled iron, metal, rags, paper, bottles. "It was a junk shop," Bernard Schapiro remembered:

> People came to us with loaded push carts and horse wagon rigs. We sorted the material and sold it to wholesalers. But we planned to stay in the business only long enough to learn the language and then go back into the sales of woolen piece goods, the same business we were in when I was growing up in Austria.
>
> After an easy life in Europe, we had to work in an unheated plant with a cold, cobblestone floor. My father owned the business and my brother Joe and I helped out after school. He never paid us. We put rags on our feet during the coldest part of the winter. It was so cold our knuckles would bleed.

When Joe was twenty, the brothers decided to open their own shop, specializing in rags and cloth. Bernard noted, "We wanted to specialize in the the rags and cloth business because it was cheaper, it took less capital. Also, we didn't want to stay in the 'filthy' end of the business. We wanted to better ourselves.

"My brother had just gotten out of the army and although our father, Solomon, disagreed with us, we named the business after him, 'S. Schapiro and Sons,' starting on Low Street near Aisquith. We moved three times in the next few years, from one narrow street to another, to improve our facilities."

By 1921, Solomon Schapiro decided his business was too much work without his sons. Bernard said: "He got out and went into the real estate business. We took over his place on Forrest Street, and in 1927 greatly expanded. We moved to a building close to a railroad siding on Caroline Street.

"We bought a new building and got into new materials, even though we couldn't pay off our bank loan."

IMMIGRANTS Kalman and Anna Hettleman arrived in Baltimore as their port of entry (at Locust Point) in 1902 from Russia with their two children, William and Isidore, eight-ninths of another (who would be David), and, according to the reminiscence of the late Emanuel Hettleman recorded for the Jewish Museum of Maryland, "not much else." Emanuel Hettleman himself was born two years later, in 1904, on Low Street. It was, as he told the story years later, "February 13, 1904, six days after the Great Baltimore Fire. We were very poor. . . . We had only outdoor plumbing and we lived on the third floor, and my brothers and I slept on blankets on the floor."

A few years later, the family was able to move to somewhat better accommodations at 39 South Bond Street. "Among our new neighbors were the Bronsteins, who had a rag factory on the corner," Emanuel's account continues. The proximity of that rag factory would help shape the life and times of the Hettlemans more than they could have known at the time:

> Mr. Bronstein would go out and peddle for junk. He'd bring it into his shop and then go out and resell it. He seemed to progress, and was soon renting pushcarts to peddlers who would go out for him, down the same streets and alleys, and bring the stuff back. These peddlers would go out in the morning and come back late in the afternoon with pushcarts full of junk. My father watched how that worked, and in 1904, the year I was born, he bought what he used to call "a rag, bone and bottle shop" at 1218 Bank Street. It was a hole in the wall.
>
> The name started as "Kalman Hettleman and Sons, Inc.," which was the name my father used when he founded the business, and it stayed that way, while my older brother Isidore and I together built the business.

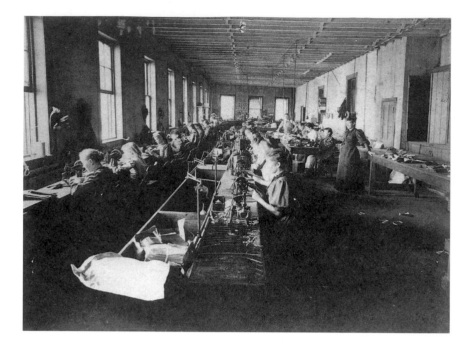

The Hess Shoe Company factory at Fayette and Harrison Streets, about 1900. Nathan Hess founded the company in 1872 to manufacture shoes, but before the third decade in the century the firm had given itself over to retailing. The Hess name disappeared from Baltimore retailing in 1999, after fitting Baltimoreans for their shoes for 127 years.

THE SCRAP INDUSTRY in Baltimore included many other companies, most of which were all Jewish, most of which could trace their roots to dealing off the streets of Baltimore. For example, Morris Schapiro (Boston Iron and Metals) had two brothers, Jacob and Isaac. I. D. Shapiro, son of Jacob, recounted the family history:

> My father landed in Baltimore at the age of fourteen from a seasick voyage in steerage across the Atlantic. His two brothers were here and already established in the junk business. Jacob worked in his brothers' junkyards. As a laborer, he learned what junk preparation was, and that there was a difference between iron and other metals such as copper.
>
> He saw no future in what he was doing in his brothers' scrap yards, so he did what other scrap peddlers did in those days: He rented a horse and wagon for a dollar a day, and picked up metals whenever he could find them. One of his early purchases was the iron fence around the Green Mount Cemetery.
>
> From a small junk shop around Aisquith Street he moved to a large tract of land in Southwest Baltimore on Wilkens Avenue. There he modernized. After World War I, scrap became a recognized commodity and the dealers' businesses grew with this recognition. There are no "junk" dealers today. They are "recyclers." They were that before the term came into the language.

SAMUEL KAHAN, president of Ansam Metals Corporation, a firm that has become one of the larger businesses in Baltimore's scrap industry today, reflects:

> The spectacular growth of Baltimore's scrap business is a story that grew out of the ancient prejudice against Jews. In the America in which they found themselves, there were strong prejudices that kept them out of the respectable professions and businesses. They could only go into businesses that were degrading and the junkyard business was one of them. They did not choose to be junk peddlers, they were forced to be.
>
> But yesterday's "rag, bones and bottles" collectors became the "alloyers" and the smelters and refiners that make up the giant recycling industry of today. That part, what the industry now does, has changed. But what hasn't is the Jewish identity of the business. It has been more than three-quarters of a century since the founding families started their junk businesses, and the industry by any measure is still mostly Jewish.
>
> And the Jewish community has benefited from the success of this peculiarly Jewish industry. It has provided communal leaders like Morton Plant, chief executive officer of Keywell Corp. and a descendant of the Klaff family. The community has been the beneficiary of philanthropy from the scrap industry in amounts that cannot be counted.

Not bad for families whose forebears started life in this country scratching out a living by picking up junk in the alleys of old East Baltimore.

Hanover Street Wholesalers: A World of Their Own

"The street came alive at 8:00 every morning but was pretty well shut down during Jewish holidays."

A 1938 Chamber of Commerce report stated that the business of wholesaling in Baltimore "was at an all-time high." During the year, the group's data showed, "932 merchants from Baltimore, Western Maryland, and the Eastern shore purchased a total of $992,571 in goods, an average of $1,064 per buyer" (all in 1938 dollars). They bought a variety of items at wholesale prices: ladies' dresses, cigars and tobacco, neckwear, shoes, rubber goods, hats and caps, men's clothing and furnishings, window shades and draperies. Most of these wholesale houses were concentrated in the

Hanover Street area, between Baltimore and Lombard Streets, and most of them were Jewish-owned.

Askin Brothers, Inc., wholesalers of hosiery and underwear, was at 13 South Hanover Street. Ira Askin remembers going down to work there when he was as young as fourteen. "Especially during holiday times," he recalls, "I would help with the packing. Wednesday afternoons were particularly busy times on Hanover Street in those days because all of the merchants in the small towns surrounding Baltimore—Hagerstown, Frederick, Cumberland in Western Maryland, and Salisbury and many of the small towns on the Eastern Shore—would close their stores, and use that time to come to Baltimore and spend time on Hanover Street, buying.

"The wholesalers were mostly Jewish, with one or two exceptions. They were from the old time, Eastern European school of hard work and long hours. Many chose to be wholesalers because they would not have to open their businesses on Saturday, the Jewish Sabbath. 'Closed Saturday' was the custom of the wholesaling trade. They could remain *shomrei shabbos*."

The gathering places of this Eastern European merchants' village were Kruger's restaurant at 229 East Baltimore Street, the Dinner Bell at Redwood and Charles Streets, and the Triangle between Baltimore and Lombard on Hanover Street. Over bagels and coffee or hot roast beef sandwiches on rye, the members of this fraternity would gather to talk about sports and the events of the day, but mostly to talk *gesheft*.

Kruger's closed its doors on April 3, 1960. Late on that fateful day, Ira remembers, a dozen or so of the Hanover Street merchants who had pa-

Henry Sonneborn and Company's factory workers, ca. 1910. Sonneborn came to Baltimore in 1849, when he was twenty-three years old, and by the first decade of the twentieth century, the company advertised itself as "the largest clothing factory in the world, manufacturing 3,000 suits daily." In the 1920s Sonneborn was one of the chief employers in Baltimore, ranking with Bethlehem Steel. The family, of course, lived on Eutaw Place.

In his New York apartment in 1945, Rudolf Sonneborn, son of Siegmund Sonneborn, who had been associated with the Sonneborn clothing business in Baltimore, hosted a clandestine meeting attended by fifteen American businessmen and Zionist leaders. They had heard a report from David Ben Gurion on the perilous state of European Jewry. At this meeting, the "*Exodus 1947*" project was born.

tronized the place for years, into the second generation, gathered to sing "Auld Lang Syne" to Harry Kruger. They sang a farewell to a wholesale district institution.

Julian "Sonny" Marcus worked for his family-owned wholesale shoe business, MARCO, beginning the day after he graduated from high school in 1940. His younger brother, Morton, joined the company in 1946, after graduating from high school and spending time in the service. The business had occupied the five-floor warehouse at 27 South Hanover Street since 1932. "We had no less than six shoe wholesalers in the one short block," Morton says.

M. Pearl, Morris, Joe Loew's Boston Shoe, S. Kola and D. Myers, and ourselves. We took in shoes manufactured in New England and sold them to individual stores in the entire area, as far away as the Carolinas and throughout Western Maryland and the Eastern Shore.

In my day, I worked six and seven days a week. I would start with breakfast with the guys at a restaurant called the Triangle at Hanover and Lombard Streets. Unlike many wholesale districts serving other industries, the sidewalks up and down Hanover Street were clear of merchandise. That was because each warehouse had a chute off the sidewalk, and merchandise being delivered was thrown into the chute where it wound up inside, down in basement storage areas.

I came back to Hanover Street after the war. But by 1956 or so the word was on the street that the city and the federal government wanted the land to build the Mechanic Theatre complex and the federal office building. So the big exodus of wholesalers off of Hanover Street was on, and by 1965, it was all over. The wrecking crews began knocking the whole place down. The businesses, the buildings and the people have all moved on. The street of the Jewish wholesalers lives only in the memories of the men—mostly men—who worked there. There aren't many of us left.

Among the dwindling group of Hanover Street's alumni is Leonard Sachs, whose family owned the Jess Company, wholesalers of ladies' dresses at 6 South Hanover Street. He remembers that commotion was constant on the sidewalk in front of the three-story Jess Company building as trucks unloaded merchandise from the New York manufacturers, wheeling the loaded racks from curbside into the company's warehouse. "I have great memories of going up Hanover and Fayette at lunch time and taking a wire cage elevator up to Klein's Billiard Parlor for the best roast beef sandwiches on earth and a quiet game of pool in a dimly lit pool parlor restaurant. I went with Ira Askin, Nat Levy, Morton Cohen, Jerry Hartz and Stanley Hartz. We all got our haircuts at the Lord Baltimore Barber Shop, down in the lower lobby."

IT WAS RAINING on a morning in August of 1997 when Julian Marcus, on a sentimental journey back to the Hanover Street that is no more, stood in front of the Lord Baltimore Hotel, looking south, wistfully, across the street towards the complex of buildings that included the Mechanic and the Mechanic Plaza, the Mercantile Safe Deposit and Trust Building, and the federal courthouse. He had come to this place (at this writer's request) to transport himself back almost thirty years to the geography and times of the South Hanover Street he knew as a boy and a young man. Now he was seeing those buildings and walkways and plaza and fountains occupying hallowed ground, the same few square blocks of the city where a couple dozen (mostly Jewish) merchants and their customers once made up a milling populace engaged in the historically Jewish role of wholesaling, operating "in between" the manufacturer and the retailer. In those vanished buildings and lost streets, Sonny Marcus and Ira Askin and Leonard Sachs and so many young Jewish men of their generation had invested so much of their lives.

"Right about there," Mr. Marcus said, pointing to the far end of the Mechanic, "is where MARCO Shoe was, 27 South Hanover, just below Redwood. Askin's was just to the north of us. I can still see the big tractor-trailers stopping in the street to unload, and traffic working its way around them.

"The street came alive about eight in the morning and was busy up to around five-thirty. Just before Easter was the busiest time, because so many of the wholesalers sold hats and shoes and women's clothing. But on Yom Kippur and the first day of Rosh Hashanah—I think only Max and Wolpert and one or two others closed both days—you could shoot a cannon down the street and hit no one."

He was a man walking through a memory. Of the look and feel of that storied street—the merchants, the merchandise, Klein's Billiard Parlor, the Lord Baltimore Hotel Barber Shop, Kruger's Restaurant—of those places and times, all that remain are stories and a dwindling cadre of aging Hanover Street alumni to share them.

Hendler's: The Man, the Legend, the Ice Cream

Mannie Hendler helped define his times.

In the windows of drugstores, confectioneries and groceries, and on the yellow trucks criss-crossing Baltimore, you saw it everywhere, the familiar trademarked Kewpie doll with a vague come-hither look, advertising "Hendler's, the Velvet Kind." From the start of the century through the 1960s, Hendler's Ice Cream was among the most widely recognized and wildly popular brand names in Baltimore. L. Manuel "Mannie" Hendler himself, the firm's founder, was well known and respected both within and beyond the local Jewish community.

Almost forty years after his death, his memory endures: the board room of the Jewish Museum of Maryland, for example, is a re-creation of Hendler's old office in the ice cream plant, a handsome brick building still located at 1100 East Baltimore Street. There's still a Hendler Lane at Eutaw Place, running alongside the lot in which the Hendler mansion once stood. Hendler's signs are collectors' items, adorning family dens all over town.

Who was Lionel Manuel Hendler? Why and how did his name and ice cream become such enduring Baltimore institutions?

Although Mr. Hendler furnished information about his life many times for biographies in various publications, he revealed precious little about his childhood. He never stated where he was born. He never said more about his schooling than "public, high, Baltimore County." Nor did he ever note that he was a member in excellent standing of both the Chizuk Amuno and the Baltimore Hebrew Congregations; he listed his religious affiliation, when it was called for, as "Jewish Conservative."

From news clippings, documents, and people's memories, however, one is able to piece together a fuller biography, though it is not necessarily authoritative, and certainly remains anecdotal. L. Manuel Hendler was born February 10, 1885, at 3738 Bank Street, to Isaac and Belle Sachs Hendler. Isaac Hendler operated a dairy in East Baltimore at several locations, according to city directories. An 1890 picture of the family shows Isaac and five-year-old L. Manuel seated on a horse, surrounded by family members Reuben and Bluma Sachs, Billie Sachs Hendler, and Bernard Hendler, along with several workmen.

Family lore holds that young L. Manuel worked in his father's dairy store and saw a future in an offshoot of the dairy trade, the fledgling business of manufacturing ice cream. (Ice cream had a special presence in Baltimore because the business, on a large-scale commercial basis at any rate, was started here by a Jacob Fussell.) In 1905, Hendler, only twenty, founded his own ice cream business in what a news report called a "a tiny plant on Lloyd Street."

Mr. Hendler must have felt optimistic about the future, because he got married—on December 9, 1906, to Rose Duke. They had four children: Bernice, Albert, Florence, and Naomi. In 1912, Mr. Hendler moved his business to a grand brick plant at 1100 East Baltimore Street, a testimony to its spectacular growth. At this time, Hendler's Creamery was capitalized at a hundred thousand dollars. Its new plant, the former powerhouse of the old Baltimore City Passenger Railway Company at Baltimore Street and tiny East Street, cost forty thousand dollars.

From there on out, Hendler was a household word in Baltimore. The company's Kewpie doll trademark became widely recognized, its famous flavors became the stuff of conversation. At its peak, the company had distribution in 400 stores, served by a fleet of 120 delivery trucks.

About those flavors, Albert Hendler, who went to work for his father when he was sixteen and retired as company president in 1966, recalled:

When the Howard Johnson company began advertising twenty-eight flavors, I became curious to know how many we had. So I sent one of our men down to the storage room to check the numbers. We had over fifty flavors in stock.

Not all were big sellers, but we kept all in inventory for certain customers. For example, we supplied Hutzler's with ginger and peppermint, which were featured regularly on their menu, though those

Many of Baltimore's Jewish entrepreneurs, following the centuries-old tradition of acting as "middlemen," became successful wholesalers. Joseph M. Zamoiski was born in London, England, in 1858. He was the son of Jacob Zamoiski, who had left Poland at an early age for London. He lived there until 1860, when he emigrated to the United States. Son Joseph Zamoiski came to America when he was five years old, in 1863. In 1896, after owning and successfully operating his own electrical supply business, Joseph Zamoiski founded one of Baltimore's first Jewish-owned wholesale companies, which later became one of the region's largest and is still in business today. The Zamoiskis also figure in local radio history. Joseph's son Calman obtained one of the first three licenses to broadcast in Baltimore in 1922—for station WKC, broadcasting from the stable behind his home at 2527 Madison Avenue.

flavors did not sell well in the drugstores. For a few schools we made grapenut ice cream. We also made a licorice, and date-coffee, which contained chopped dates. Also spice apple, and walnut-sized walnuts, which came packaged in a wooden bowl, in the center of which was an actual English walnut. Also "cherigold" vanilla with maraschino cherries.

But the best flavor was tomato aspic, which we made as a specialty for the Southern Hotel. It was served as a staple with the main course at dinner. Eggnog ice cream was one of our best sellers. It was flavored with pure rum, which we put in bonded warehouses for three years. To my knowledge, we were the only ice cream company in the nation to have a liquor or rectifier's license for the blending of whiskey for other than drinking purposes.

As L. Manuel Hendler's business grew, so did his presence in the community. He held board positions in the secular and civic communities: the Red Cross, Boy Scouts, United Palestine Appeal, Associated Jewish Charities, Joint Distribution Committee; Association of Ice Cream Manufacturers, and the Borden Company, which had owned the Hendler Creamery since 1929. And every Christmas season Hendler's received deserved recognition for donating ice cream to orphanages and hospital wards.

The Hendlers lived in a mansion at 913 Lake Drive at Eutaw Place and enjoyed life at both the Woodholme and Suburban country clubs. They summered at their waterfront home, "Harlequin on the Severn." L. Manuel Hendler retired in June of 1961 and died after a short illness the following year. The funeral was at the Jack Lewis Funeral Home at North Avenue and Eutaw Place; Rabbi Israel Goldman of Chizuk Amuno officiated. The Hendler ice cream name lived a little longer; it was retired in 1971.

The Hendler's Kewpie doll signs are gone, now the province of nostalgia buffs and flea market shoppers. The name and the legend invite revisiting by those interested in the Hendler legacy—an extraordinary product created and marketed by an extraordinary man. And because the family name was also the name of product, "Hendler" the man and "Hendler" the ice cream ("Take home a brick!") are fused in the community psyche.

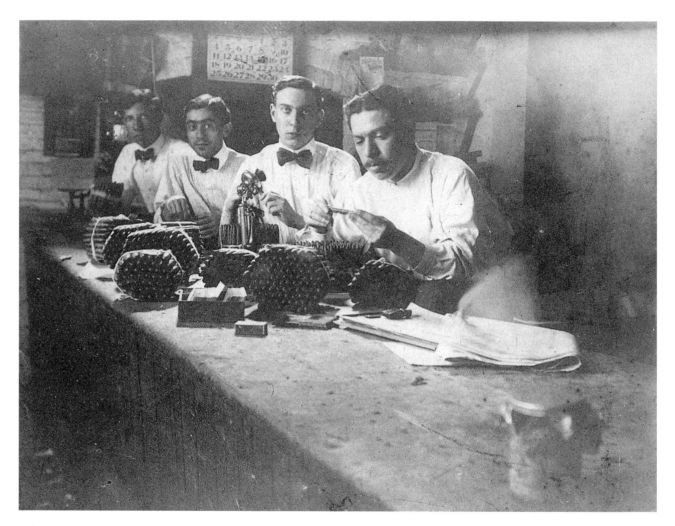

Heineman Brothers Cigar Factory, on the southeast corner of Eastern Avenue and Exeter Streets, ca. 1905. Five brothers were in the business—Samuel S., Jesse S., Mortimer S., Milton S., and Bertram S. Heineman.

JOSEPH WIESENFELD
Little Joe Wiesenfeld Co., Sporting Goods

"Little Joe" Wiesenfeld (he was under five feet) as he appeared in a volume that flattered the aspiring with whimsical caricature, *Clubman of Maryland* (1915). Proprietor of "Little Joe's," one on the northwest corner of Howard and Baltimore Streets and the other at 14 North Howard Street, Wiesenfeld sold camping and fishing gear, bicycles, toys, sports gear, electric trains, and saddlery, and for a short time, automobiles—he tried to sell everything the department stores did not. Joe's son, Moses, operates the second car, a roadster that dates the photograph to about the same time the book of sketches appeared.

Next door, *below*, is the clothing factory of the Baltimore Bargain House. A sign directs customers to the firm's sales rooms at 204-20 West Baltimore Street. A seventeen-year-old immigrant, Jacob Epstein, had founded the Baltimore Bargain House when he came to America in 1882. He could barely speak the language. In 1929, when the family sold the business, it was one of the largest of its kind in America. Peddlers carried Baltimore Bargain House merchandise to small towns all over the South, and more than a few of the travelers stayed in the South and opened small shops that became giant department stores.

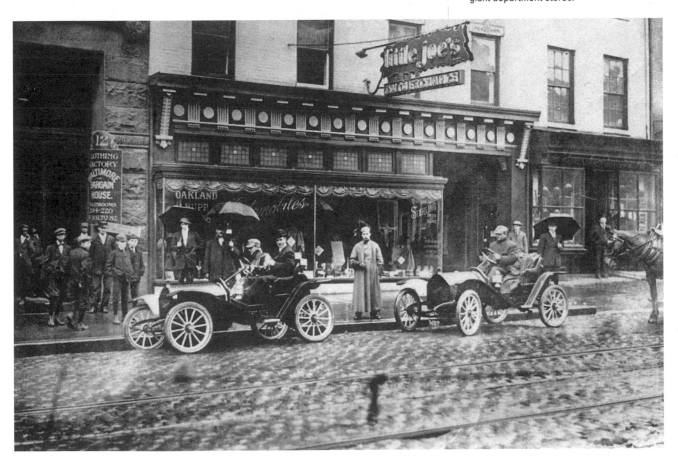

The Broadway Bargain House, ca. 1920,
when Max Aaron Cohen (on the right)
opened the store at 624-26 South Broadway.
Flower pots above the canopy added a dash
of greenery. Cohen was also a ship chan-
dler. His son, Samuel Max Cohen (*left*), continued in the retail trade, operating Cohen's
Men's Wear. The store remains in business
at the Yorktowne Shopping Center, Cock-
eysville.

Abraham and Samuel Askin established a hosiery and underwear wholesaling firm in 1915, using a sturdy truck to deliver merchandise from their shop at 133 Aisquith Street to retailers throughout the region. A photographer captured the brothers and assistants inside a new shop at 18 South Hanover Street in 1932, when the Askin Brothers Company joined the concentration of wholesale houses—most of them Jewish owned—on Hanover between Baltimore and Lombard Streets. Wednesday afternoons tended to be particularly busy because merchants from places like Hagerstown, Frederick, Cumberland, and Salisbury would close shop and come to Hanover Street to do their buying. *Left to right:* Gilbert Wallace, William Sheely, Abraham Askin, George Durkin, George Frank, Samuel Askin, Herman Moog. The Askin Brothers Company stayed in business until 1986.

The Hecht Company traces its origins to 1857, when Samuel Hecht, a one-time peddler in the city and on the Eastern Shore, went into business on Aliceanna Street, near Broadway in Fells Point. His wife, Babette Wolfsheimer, and four sons, Emanuel, Albert, Alexander, and Moses, all became active in the business. Over the years Hecht's expanded throughout Baltimore and into Washington and Annapolis. This architecturally interesting Hecht Brothers Building at Baltimore and Pine Streets, pictured in about 1930, primarily handled credit furniture and clothing sales. Over the years, besides Hecht Brothers at Howard and Lexington (known as Hecht-May), Howard and Franklin, and Baltimore and Pine, Hecht's operated the Hub at Charles and Fayette Streets, and Hecht's Reliable and Hecht's Broadway, both in Fells Point.

In 1957 the management included Samuel Hecht, grandson of the founder and chairman of the board; Robert H. Levi, president; and J. Jefferson Miller, executive vice president.

The giant downtown department store windows were not just displays of merchandise, they were theater. Much thought and imagination (and expense) went into their creation, and in this competition Hochschild's and Hutzler's were always among the leaders. The "Christmas windows" were the apogee of the window dresser's art. Hutzler's, Hochschild's, Stewart's, and the Hecht Company vied to create the most talked-about and crowd-pulling displays at Howard and Lexington Streets. The displays offered laughing Santas, singing choir boys, flying angels, and busy elves making toys and working on Santa's sleigh. Here we see one of Hutzler's windows featuring Walt Disney's Pinocchio, as well as eager onlookers gathering for a peek at another scene. (Courtesy of the Maryland Historical Society.)

In 1938 Hutzler's celebrated its eightieth anniversary with windows carrying historical motifs, including a diorama of the legendary race on the B&O tracks between a horse-drawn passenger car and the steam locomotive *Tom Thumb.*

Howard Burman first published the *Home News, the People's Paper,* in January 1938, and the weekly soon became a favorite in the Jewish community. Here, in the paper's own window, Burman invites passersby to take special note of his July advertisers' products—Esskay, Blue Ribbon, Crosse and Blackwell, and Suburban Club ("Means Quality") soft drinks. *Home News* ownership passed to the Maryland Broadcasting Company in 1949. At its peak, the paper boasted circulation of 120,000 homes. It ceased publication in 1954.

Under a supervisor's watchful eye in the 1930s, women at dozens of sewing machines make cotton frocks for the Merrygarden Company, owned by the A. S. Katzenberg and Brothers family. At the time, in the middle of the Depression, employees were happy to get work.

The first floor interior of Isaac Hamburger and Sons men's clothing store, in 1939. The building's first floor featured men's shoes, hats, and furnishings; the second, sportswear and boy's clothing; the third, men's clothing. The remaining five floors were used for manufacturing until 1922, when Hamburgers went out of the manufacturing business.

Hess Shoes' Baltimore Street storefront, ca. 1940, elegant with its art deco look. Hess also owned a complex of buildings on Howard Street but branched out from downtown with much success. A generation of Baltimoreans still talk about Hess's store at York and Belvedere, which not only sold shoes but offered children a sliding board and a place ("the Snippery") to get their hair cut. At its Edmondson Village store, Hess created a "monkey house," complete with the antics of four wooly ringtail monkeys from Brazil. In 1979, the family business was sold to the Goertz Corporation of Hamburg, West Germany. At the time, Hess had sixteen stores in Baltimore and Washington.

A Hendler's Ice Cream billboard and a truck
on service rounds during World War II. At
its peak, the company had 120 delivery
trucks supplying Hendler's ice cream
("The Velvet Kind") to 400 stores.

Hutzler's mounted an Aaron Sopher exhibit to celebrate the store's ninetieth year in 1948. In the 1930s Sopher worked at his studio on the southwest corner of Charles and Madison Streets, next door to what was once the Stafford Hotel. He enjoyed a reputation for producing artwork quickly—but also well—usually people, caricatured in social situations. Many Jewish families still hold on to their "Sophers." His friend and contemporary Jacob Glushakow said, "He would always get it right the first time. He used to ride the streetcar from his home on Fernwood Avenue in Forest Park to his studio and draw things he saw from his seat. I saw him sit in Bickford's restaurant on Calvert Street and draw people at another table. He'd stick his thumb in his coffee and then apply it to the drawing. The effect was to wash the drawing with a kind of sepia tone." Besides Glushakow, Sopher's circle of fellow Jewish artists included Eddie Rosenfeld, Herman Maril, Mervin Jules, Reuben Kramer, Selma Oppenheimer, Florence Hochschild Austrian, and Helen Reis.

Isaac Hamburger and Sons held its centennial dinner at the Southern Hotel in November 1950, a gathering that included the store's African American employees, at a time when integration in retailing was uncommon.

At the head table, *clockwise from left:* Robert Berney, Sidney Berney, Betty Hamburger, Merle Hamburger, Gretchen Berney, Edwin Aaronson, Max Hochschild, Henry Hamburger, Governor Herbert R. O'Conor, advertising executive Joseph Katz (standing at podium), Jonas Hamburger, Isaac Hamburger II, and Dorothy Berney. Eleven years later, as part of the Charles Center renewal plan, Hamburger's moved to Charles Street, occupying an odd building that bridged Fayette Street. The family sold the business to Van Heusen in 1968.

Motoring chic and television sets
(black and white) took center
stage in Hutzler's windows during
the 1950s. Hutzler's held its share
in television retailing at the time;
discount houses like Luskin's later
took their own share of that business.

Join the Crusade for
Freedom

Through the 1950s and into the early 1960s, Hutzler's men's clothing department competed successfully with the prestigious men's wear speciality stores by offering exclusive lines, such as the renowned Oxxford suits.

Moses Shaivitz founded his furniture company at 816 South Charles Street in 1891.
The family history holds that soon after the
turn of the century both his sons, Sol and
Henry, quit school to join the business,
which asked customers simply to "Look for
the clock in the middle of the block."

A view of Howard and Saratoga Streets looking south in the 1960s, when a decline in the old retail district had become hard to deny. Meanwhile, Hess Shoes used taxicabs to advertise a new store in Reisterstown Road Plaza. Mano Swartz furriers and Stewart's department store stand in the distance, on the east side of Howard Street. In the vicinity, though not visible in this picture, was another Baltimore institution—Awrach and Perl's delicatessen at 223 North Howard Street, luncheon headquarters for many a Saturday shopper. A menu from the 1940s lists sixteen omelets, forty-seven sandwiches, plus a variety of steaks and chops, and European delicacies such as schmaltz herring. The owners were two immigrants from Odessa.

In the 1950s and 1960s, many downtown retailers bowed to necessity and followed their customers to the suburbs. The first department store to open suburban branches was Hochschild, Kohn, and Company, first at Edmondson Village and then at York Road and Belvedere Avenue. Isaac Hamburger and Sons opened its first suburban branch store on York Road in 1964. Other Hamburgers branch store openings followed: Westview, Eastpoint, and Reisterstown Road Plaza. Hutzler's opened this store in White Marsh in 1981. As the Jewish community moved out of the city and into the north and west suburbs, so did the stores catering to them, as well as the synagogues and the institutions serving the Jewish community.

The Way We Were

Pimlico: The Track and the Neighborhood

Pimlico the sports destination and Pimlico the neighborhood would always be bound together.

In 1868, Pimlico (the track) was carved out of Pemlicoe (the tract). The decision had come about at a dinner party two years earlier, where Maryland Governor Oden Bowie found himself a guest among fellow racing enthusiasts at the Union Hall Hotel in Saratoga, then the posh playground of the rich in upstate New York. The country had come through a civil war in which the horse racing fraternity had been, like so many other institutions, devastated. The group had gathered among their own to discuss where to build a state-of-the-art track, to bring their beloved sport of kings back to its proper place. But Governor Bowie, though seemingly mixing it up with the boys and appearing open to their ideas, had his own plan to build a track in Maryland. Before the evening was over, the Governor's will had prevailed. The racetrack would be built in Baltimore's Pemlicoe area and would come to be known as Pimlico.

A few years later, on the sunlit afternoon of October 26, 1870, the horses broke from the starting gate at Pimlico, signaling a Baltimore first. That inaugural race was named after the dinner party at which the idea of the track was conceived— "The Dinner Party Stakes" (later called "The Dixie Handicap"). Its winner was named "Preakness." Governor Bowie, seated in the grandstand, must have been smiling.

Three years later, on May 27, 1873, twelve thousand people cheered the first Preakness Stakes at Pimlico. On that long-ago day, the track became midwife to the small village born nearby at Belvedere and Park Heights Avenues. Pimlico the sports destination and Pimlico the neighborhood would always be bound together.

Among the troops pictured here at the Baltimore Jewish Welfare Agency at Camp Meade in 1917 was a young soldier in the Army Quartermaster Corps, Lester Levy (a relative of whom took the photograph). Members of the Baltimore Jewish community operated the center as a place for the men to socialize with other soldiers of the same faith and attend Jewish services. Levy and Leslie W. Moses were grandsons of M. (Michael) S. Levy, who began manufacturing straw hats as early as 1878; by the mid-1890s he had taken all his sons, William, Jacob, Julius, and Alfred, into the business. Until the 1960s, when the men's hat business melted away, M. S. Levy and Sons ranked among the largest manufacturers of men's straw hats in the world and made Baltimore the nation's center for the "straw hat." Lester Levy carried on his family's tradition of philanthropy—and also became renowned for his distinguished collection of American sheet music.

By the 1930s Pimlico was already a thriving commercial center, beginning (arbitrarily) on the 4900 block of Park Heights Avenue. Depending on the year, this first block was dominated by Luskin's and the Park Heights Bowling Alley. In the 5000 block were Shure's Pharmacy and the Uptown Theater. The Uptown opened in 1941, with *Sunny*, starring Anna Neagle and John Carroll. In 1974 it was operating on a reduced schedule and by 1975 had closed altogether.

On the 5100 block were Rabai's and Silber's bakeries, Arundel Ice Cream Parlor, and Slater's food market. Slater's opened in 1940 and remained in business until 1980. Mrs. Rhona Slater Block, Hyman Slater's daughter, recalls, "Our store was open seven days a week, fifty-two weeks a year, from early in the morning until midnight. Every other food market in town could be closed, but not Slater's. Slater's was open. My mother Tillie, my sister Shirley Ravitz, and behind the meat counter for maybe twenty-five years, Hyman Rabinowitz, worked right alongside my father."

The Pimlico movie theater stood at 5132 Park Heights Avenue. It opened in 1914; its last show, on September 8, 1952, was *The Redhead and the Cowboy*, with Rhonda Fleming. Abe Snyder's men's clothing was at 5136. Mr. Snyder was so much a part of Pimlico for so long that he became known as "Mr. Pimlico." His daughter, Mrs. Estelle Snyder Kahn, says, "My sisters,

Lester Levy and his fellow soldiers in tented field and prepared to move out.

Phyllis Snyder Kane and Ethel Snyder Goldfein, and I worked there dressing and undressing the windows. We sold in 1943 to Reamer's."

Pleet's deli was at 5144; Beeli's pharmacy was at 5145 at the corner of Belvedere; Little Jeff's men's clothing was at the corner of 5200; Lipnick's hardware at 5216, and Gundy's gift shop at 5217. Gundy's, founded in 1939 by Jean Gundersheimer, was bought by Ruth Nachman in 1953. Patrons remember Gundy's as upscale, offering platters, bowls, canisters, stationery, gift cards and wrapping, ice buckets, linens, and guest towels. Ms. Nachman moved Gundy's out of Pimlico in 1961. "The reputation of the store," Ms. Nachman says, "brought customers into Pimlico from all over Baltimore."

The people who came "from all over Baltimore to Pimlico" came, for the most part—particularly in the 1930s and 1940s—by streetcar. Streetcars ran minutes apart, lumbering up and down Park Heights Avenue and across Belvedere Avenue. The Numbers 5 and 33 streetcars carried passengers north to Pimlico and West Arlington along Belvedere Avenue. Before 1932, the Number 5 ran all the way out Park Heights to Reisterstown and Emory Grove. The line was cut back to terminate at Park Heights and Manhattan Avenues, just above Belvedere, where it connected to a bus service.

The Pimlico Hotel restaurant opened at 5301 Park Heights Avenue in 1952. Though some may have thought of it as "Nates and Leon's North," it certainly wasn't. The Pimlico Hotel was not conceived to be another Nates and Leon's, which in its day—from 1937 to the mid-1960s—was easily Northwest Baltimore's most popular delicatessen restaurant. The Pimlico Hotel was planned to be a first-class, white tablecloth restaurant. And it was. The Pimlico Hotel offered a fourteen-page menu, more than one hundred entrees, a complete Chinese menu, a full page of "suggestions" that changed daily, and hot steamed crabs. On weekends, more than 180 people helped prepare and serve as many as 1,000 meals a day.

But the Pimlico Hotel will be remembered, too, for its Cavalier Lounge ("Live Music Every Night!"). Park Heights' famous Pimlico Hotel closed in 1984. The nightlife reviewers Chapin and Chapin paid a visit to the Hotel's Cavalier Lounge one night in 1977: "These people are more interested in meeting someone of the same outlook and background than in drinking or dancing. Ladies in search of doctor and lawyer husbands can take heart— the men here generally outnumber the women. . . . Speaking of dancing, at the Pimlico it is not up to the standards, say, of any of the disco places."

The gourmet delicatessen of Louis Kahn and his son Henry was at 5317 Park Heights Avenue. Former customer Joan Strouse Sandler recalled that

Henry Kahn worked hard at his role, which he saw as tastemaker for the German Jewish families who had moved from Eutaw Place to Mt. Washington and upper Park Heights. He took a paternal pride in recommending such delicacies as cocktail onions, olives, imported cheeses, cold cuts, liverwurst, sliced ham, chocolate marshmallow cookies, white asparagus, cornichons (miniature French pickles), and Russian caviar. Nancy Patz Blaustein remembered her frequent trips to Kahn's this way: "Mr. Kahn the elder would sit me on top of a pretzel tin and feed me samples of homemade pickles, bologna, seeded rye bread with mustard. Perched on top of a pretzel tin in Henry Kahn's was heaven."

Of all the commercial centers that had developed along the Park Heights corridor in its golden age, from Park Circle to Rogers Avenue, Pimlico was the largest, the busiest, and the most diverse (even offering two movie houses). The prestige surrounding its very name prompted many businessmen and residents, up through the 1930s, to use "Pimlico, Md." as part of their addresses.

The Streetcars of Northwest Baltimore: Ties That Bound

"I had a date once who took me downtown on the streetcar on New Year's Eve!"

Before the automobile culture, a generation of young Northwest Baltimoreans depended on streetcars to get to school, to get downtown to the movies and the Hippodrome stage shows, to go shopping, to dance classes, to the Peabody and the Pratt, and to wherever young dating couples traveled. Run these clanging streetcars in reverse, back through enough years, and they connect to a remembered time and place.

Park Heights Avenue runs north from Park Circle at Reisterstown Road to well beyond the city line. From the 1920s through the 1950s it was served by the Numbers 5 and 33 streetcar lines; Liberty Heights runs from its junction at Reisterstown Road at Mondawmin out to Baltimore County where it becomes Liberty Road and runs west forever; the Liberty Heights stretch was served by the Number 32 (and connecting to it, the Number 31, running along Garrison Boulevard). The Number 25 ran along Ken Oak Road and then onto Falls Road, linking Mt. Washington to downtown and the world.

Throughout the early 1930s, five days a week, whatever the weather, Stanley Greenebaum waited for the Number 5 at Menlo Drive and Park Heights. He recalls: "I was going to Garrison Junior High School and took the streetcar to Park Heights Avenue and Belvedere Avenue. I transferred

The Forest, 3300 Garrison Boulevard, offered the charms of neo-Moorish architecture and—in 1934—of Fredric March in *All of Me*. (Courtesy of the Enoch Pratt Free Library.)

to the Number 25 or 33, which took us to the Belvedere Avenue carbarn, and then we took the No. 31 to Garrison Boulevard and Barrington Road. I rode the same cars in reverse order coming home. We knew every conductor and every motorman, and they knew us.

"Over the years, I'd join the guys, Malcolm Rudolph, Harry Shapiro, Lenny Sachs, and go downtown on the streetcars to the movies and back." Leonard Sachs remembers that they often took streetcars to the Lakewood swimming pool, then located at Charles and Twenty-sixth Street.

Those who stayed on the Number 5 or 33 for the length of its route south would have passed through Pimlico, past the Uptown and Avalon theaters, the Shaarei Zion synagogue, the Japanese pagoda gate at Carlin's Park, and the A&W Hot Shoppe. The ride continued on down Reisterstown Road to Fulton Avenue, east to Druid Hill Avenue, and into downtown.

Helen Burman Sollins, who lived on Fairview Avenue in Forest Park, has distinct memories of catching the Number 32 at Garrison Boulevard and Liberty Heights Avenue. "We always wore white gloves, which was not unusual on the streetcars in those days. Leonard Sollins—who would later become my husband—did not have a car in the 1940s, and so we always went down and back on the Number 32."

Phyllis Cooper Schaefer also went downtown on the streetcar with Leonard, before his courtship with Helen Burman. One night in June 1941, Leonard, in tuxedo and carrying a corsage, rang the bell at 3414 Wolcott Avenue. He was calling to take Phyllis to his City College junior prom. Phyllis recalled, "He hands me the corsage and we leave. Out on the sidewalk he tells me, 'We're taking the streetcar to the Lord Baltimore Hotel.' I could have died.

"There I was, dressed in a full-skirted, white pique gown. We started walking, six, eight blocks to Liberty Heights and Garrison and I am holding up my skirt, gathered around my legs, all the way to the streetcar stop."

Leonard has a somewhat different memory of the evening. "Years later Phyllis told me that she had been embarrassed by the whole thing, but I wouldn't know why. I didn't have a car. Cabs cost seventy-five cents. Plus tip. It all seemed natural enough. Streetcars were safe, clean, pretty reliable. Besides, fare was only ten cents."

Marcia Gann Pines lived at 3217 Carlisle Avenue ("our phone number was Liberty 7849," she adds) and took the Number 31 for all thirteen of her public school years, transferring to the Number 32 to get to P.S. 64, to Garrison Junior High School, and to Forest Park High School—each in its time. She recounts:

Our dates often took us to the movies, or downtown, or uptown to the Ambassador or to the Forest, on the streetcar. In the crowd were Jane Hoffberger Silberman, Rita Goldman Wagner, Betty Davidson Rothman, May Ruth Needle Seidel, and the Axman twins, Richard and Robert. I took the streetcar often to visit one of my best girlfriends, Beverly Edelman Levin, who lived on Gwynns Falls Parkway.

Joe, whom I later married, lived at 1839 Orleans Street at the time and came to my house on the streetcar. We took the streetcar to the dances at Gwynn Oak, and I remember dancing to Vaughn Monroe.

Joe (now Judge) Pines adds, "She is telling the truth, the whole truth, and nothing but the truth—except, she forgot to mention that to get to her house I had to take two streetcars. First the No. 13. Then the 31."

The Number 25 route was the closest thing to a 1930s version of an amusement park thrill ride on a public transportation system. The car traveled quietly enough down Falls Road, but when it got to Huntington Avenue in Hampden it began racing across a dizzying high trestle and seemed to take off at a rate of speed threatening to life and limb. It would not slow down until it got to Thirty-third Street and Keswick Road. From there, back on the ground, it found its way along Maryland Avenue and into downtown.

Emily Miller Rody remembered taking the Number 25 streetcar six days a week in 1939 and 1940, as well as often in years before and after:

> The Number 25 was a floating opera. Claire Rosenbush, Natalie Bisgyer, Allene Roos, Joan Strouse—we would board at Cross Country to go either to Garrison Junior High School, or in my case, downtown to the Peabody where I took piano lessons. I traveled by myself. We all did, at age ten or eleven.
>
> When we went by the Pimlico track and the horses were running, the motorman would stop the car and let us watch.
>
> My dates often took me downtown on the streetcar. Austin Fine used to take me to lunch at Read's at Howard and Lexington, and then over to the Hippodrome on many a Saturday afternoon. I had a date once who took me downtown on the streetcar on *New Year's Eve* .

Summers "Down the Shore": A Lifestyle for Many Baltimore Jewish Families

Some were public, some were private. Many Jewish families moved down to "shore homes" on the Magothy and the Severn rivers for the entire summer— "lock, stock, and barrel."

"Down the shore" was where you would find many Jewish families on weekends and often during the entire summer season in the 1930s and 1940s. Every Sunday, families would visit the public beaches; others, private ones; still others would spend the entire summer at their own home "down the shore." If summer camps for the children was part of the lifestyle of many Jewish families, summers down the shore for the family was part of the lifestyle for many others.

The public beaches included Tolchester, Bay Shore, Fort Smallwood, Bay Ridge, and Fairview.

Tolchester Beach was on the Eastern Shore in Kent County, and it was easily the most popular of the public beaches among the Jewish community. Several of the synagogues had annual Sunday excursions to Tolchester. Excursion boats (the *Tolchester*, the *Louise*, the *Emma Giles*) left the inner harbor every day for a two-hour trip across the bay to the park itself. The bay steamer *Tred Avon* carried passengers from the inner harbor twice a day, seven days a week, for a one-hour trip down the Patapsco River to the beaches of Fort Smallwood and Fairview. Both beach parks offered shaded picnic areas, food pavilions, and locker room facilities.

Bay Shore was located at Sparrows Point at the lower end of the Patapsco, east of Fort Carroll. You got there by streetcar (in most years, the Number

26). Picnickers spent the day on the beach and in the amusement park, taking in the miniature railroad, roller coaster, and midway complete with shooting galleries and penny arcades. Streetcars started leaving the city at 5:30 in the morning; the last streetcar out of Bay Shore bound for Baltimore left at 1:00 A.M.

Bay Ridge, below Annapolis at the mouth of the Severn River, could be reached only by train out of Annapolis or by steamboat out of Baltimore. It boasted a hotel, a restaurant that could seat hundreds, a boardwalk, picnic grounds, a merry-go-round, a ferris wheel, a dance pavilion, and a two-deck midway full of concession stands.

For many families, the shore home was a way of life. Joe Weisberg remembers his boyhood trips there:

I began going down to our shore [home] on the Magothy when I was twelve in the summer of 1932 and I went down there every year for forty years. When I was young and still in school, we left in June when school let out. We packed the car and off we went, down Ritchie Highway to Lipins Corner, down Mountain Road to our shore home. We would not return, save for an occasional visit back for one reason or another, until just after Labor Day.

Our first house in the early 1930s was two bedrooms with a porch, but we had so many people, friends and relatives, coming down to visit us that my father had a six bedroom house built for us.

Living summers down the shore was a way of life for us. I remember going crabbing with buddies Frank Blum and Leonard Shear. We would row over to Maga Vista beach, a public beach not far away, and sell our catch to people over there for twenty-five cents a dozen.

Reuben Shiling spent many a Sunday down the shore with his fellow club members of the Rho Delta club in 1933, 1934, and 1935. "Our club, which was formed and met at the northwest JEA, then the Isaac Davidson Hebrew School, had rented a shore home on the Severn, right across from Hendler's palatial 'Harlequin On the Severn,' and so we got around to calling our little place, which was a sort of broken-down old clapboard house in disrepair, 'Heaven on the Severn.' Actually, we used the house only to change clothes." Among his fellow club members were Reuben Pasarew, David Davidson, Isidore Pasarew, Melvin Dubin, and Nathan Paskoff. "My fondest memories of going down the shore," Mr. Shiling recalls, "were the great softball and volleyball games we had on the beach."

The Felpelstein family had a shore home on the Magothy River, near

Camp Whipporwill, the Girl Scout camp off of Mountain Road on Cockey Creek, on the approaches to Gibson Island. Milton Felpelstein reminisces:

> Our family started to go down the shore in the 1920s and we spent every summer there for about forty-five years, at least up until 1950. The house that came with the shore when we bought it was a one-story shack, but as the years went on and more and more of our family came to visit every summer, we kept adding on. We had as many as fifteen and twenty sleeping down there at one time. We had so many kids there we built bunk beds for them. It was a good life. We had a canoe and rowboat and we would go crabbing and there was always time for swimming.
>
> Other Jewish families with shores nearby included the Passans, Spectors, Weisbergs, Sakols, and Bluefelds. There were a lot of Jewish families with shore homes over at Greenhaven on Stoney Creek.

Efrem Potts and his family spent childhood summers down the shore from the time he was seven years old, in 1934, until he was twelve years old, in 1939. He recalls:

> We acquired the shore, the land, and the house, in 1934. It was a big house, too. It had eight bedrooms and on weekends every bedroom was full. We had so many guests we had them sleeping on studio couches in the living room and sun parlor.
>
> We moved down there at the end of June, lock, stock, and barrel, and stayed until late August and even into September. I remember going to Arlington Elementary school while still living down the shore. My father commuted to Baltimore six days a week to our store— "Little Potts"—on Monument Street through the entire summer. We had a small beach, our beachside was mostly pier, but we had a sixteen-foot Dodge runabout inboard motor boat that is on display today in the Chesapeake Maritime Museum. We had a lot of fun with that.
>
> There were a number of German Jewish families living in a shore community nearby that I knew as Laurel-on-Severn.

The shore Mr. Potts is talking about is "Benny Birth."

From the 1880s to well into the 1960s, the Baltimore Jewish community was divided along country-of-origin lines—German Jews and Russian Jews. The division was manifest in every aspect of family life—neighborhoods, social circles, schools, country clubs, summer camps. The separation made itself felt, too, in life down the shore: The shore of choice for a group of Baltimore German Jews in those days was called Benny Birth, a no-frills seashore club on the Severn River known officially and formally as Laurel-on-the-Severn.

Gordon "Reds" Wolman began to spend summer vacations there as a guest from the time he was six years old, in the 1930s to his mid-forties, in the 1970s. He remembers:

We called the place "Benny," although in those days I never really knew why, except that I had a vague notion the name had something to do with the "B'nai B'rith" organization. There was a clubhouse of sorts, built of lumber surplus, left over from Camp Meade and the first World War. It was an elongated building, with a men's locker room and a women's locker room, all rough hewn. There was a large open hall and dominating it was a very large stone fireplace. I recall a tiny little kitchen, and a porch with a rail around it. The porch was partially screened in and we would sit out on the open end of it, high on a bluff, and see all the way to Annapolis. I thought that it was the most beautiful spot on the Severn River.

Around the clubhouse there were about ten cottages that made up the beach community, each with its own screened-in porch. They were simply built and simply furnished. Using rollaway cots, each cottage could sleep about eight to ten people. No cottage was winterized. It got hot and it got cold and there was not much you could do about it. There was a boat house at the beach and always a number of canoes tied in it.

The families who were members included the Walter and Sidney Hollanders, the Guttmachers, the Louis Kohns, the Shakman Katzes, the Robert Goldmans, the Sidney Nyburgs, the Walter Sondheims, the Joseph Ulmans, and the Edward Halles. "Some of those families," Dr. Wolman recalled, "gave big parties down there, which struck me as miraculous, given that the facilities were so simple. I do recall that the tiny parking lot got to be crowded with long LaSalles and Packard cars."

About the name "Benny Birth": Sidney Hollander, Jr., son of one of the founders, explains, "In the 1920s there was a columnist writing for the Chicago Daily News, Finley Peter Dunne, under the pseudonym of 'Mr. Dooley.' In a column, Dunne had Dooley commenting about the

Left, facing page: The Number 5 Streetcar; and, *above*, Lower Park Heights Avenue, looking north, during the time between the two World Wars (courtesy of the Peale Museum/Maryland Historical Society). The Golden Age of Park Heights Avenue began in the 1920s. The neighborhoods along the avenue, and the streets leading off of both Park Heights Avenue and Reisterstown Road, quickly developed into Jewish neighborhoods, running north and west through the city and beyond. Among the factors that nurtured the growth of Lower Park Heights were the streetcars; the Numbers 5 and 33 ran directly downtown, when downtown was both the commercial and recreational center of Baltimore. Lower Park Heights (from Belvedere Avenue south) began to break up as a Jewish neighborhood after World War II. (Personal collection of the author.)

famous Dreyfus case and he wanted to identify Dreyfus as Jewish but apparently did not want to use the word 'Jewish.' So he, 'Dooley,' was made to remark, 'Cap'n Dreyfus was sittin' quietly in Benny Birth.' That was a corruption of B'nai B'rith, a distinctly Jewish organization. One of our members in our founding days thought it would be a lark if our gang of Jewish club members used the name and so we did. It's been 'Benny Birth' all these years."

Dr. Wolman recalls, "I remember those pleasant days and nights—we did absolutely nothing. As kids, we swam and tried to create space between sea nettles. The adults sat and talked and took in the darkening night settling in over the water that stretched all the way to the bay."

Melvin Weinman recalls what was for him the magic summer of 1939:

I was twenty years old, and working at our factory in Virginia. My family had rented a four-bedroom shore home between Crystal Beach and Forked Creek on the Magothy and I commuted back and forth on weekends. From our front porch we had an open view clear out into the Bay. We could look across the river, too, to a community called the Villas, where Stanley Sagner and his family had a shore home.

The highlight of my weekends at the shore came about because I bought a small boat for seventy-five dollars and an outboard motor for the same amount. And so every night after dinner and before dark set in I would motor over to visit a young lady at the Levin's shore. She was Bobby Levin's sister and her name was Eilene.

The war broke out before the 1940 summer season and the family decided we had best stick close to home. We never had a shore home again.

Today, many have forsaken the beach for their own pool, community swim club, or country club pool. And there are special delights to the lifestyle. But a pool is not a beach; you cannot sit by a pool with the family, in company of a small child at sunset, and together stare out across the water and watch the waves gently slapping the sand, stirring memories that link generations. The poolside life does not allow you to take a small boat at dusk across still water to call on a girl named Eilene.

The Monument Street "Y": A Home Away from Home

For hundreds of young Jewish boys and girls, the "Y" provided education and recreation.

At noon on an August day in 1933, my fourteen-year-old brother, Irving, and I, then ten, waited at Park Heights and Ulman Avenues, bathing suits and towels in hand, for the Number 5 or 33 streetcar to take us to our summer "camp," the Y at 305 West Monument Street. From several sections of the city, but particularly from Lower Park Heights, hundreds of young Jewish boys and girls were also heading toward the Y, also by streetcar.

For Baltimore's young Jewish boys and girls of the 1930s, the Young Men's and Young Women's Hebrew Association was a year-round home away from home. Small by today's standards, the Y was the forerunner of the Jewish Community Centers of both Park Heights and Owings Mills.

The Y to which these young people were drawn was a modest three-story red brick building that had been built on the empty lot owned by Johns Hopkins' McCoy College. For these sons and daughters of middle-class Eastern European families, walking into the Y was like coming into the home of an old friend, different, and separate, from the outside gentile-dominated world. The Y was conceived to be "uptown," not only in geography (west and out of East Baltimore) but also in tone and mood (with its fairly "American" courses and programming). For Jewish young people, first and second generation, it would provide a bridge to America's pluralistic society.

Entering from Monument Street, one found spacious lounges on each side of the first floor lobby. The information counter was on the right, executive offices on the left. A foyer off the lobby led to the gymnasium, described in a brochure as "36 feet in height, 53 feet, 3 inches wide and 83 feet long. The floor is marked off for basketball, indoor baseball, and volleyball. Huge windows open onto the Linden Avenue side."

The library was on the mezzanine, as were club rooms and the health club, with its "Battle Creek Universal Electric Bath cabinets, violet ray and infrared lamps, private showers, lockers, rubbing slabs and massage tables, and a private exercise room." And a reminder: "Expert masseurs are present." On the second floor was the swimming pool, the "only suspended pool in this section of the country, with seven large windows to bring in light." The pool itself was thirty feet wide and seventy-five feet long, said to be regulation American Athletic Union size, and offered two diving boards. "The pool's depth is from 3½ feet at the shallow end to 9 feet at the deep." There were six lanes for racing and a spectators' balcony. The third floor offered four of the "best handball courts in the city." Game rooms, a ping-

The YMHA basketball team, 1937-38. The popular and versatile coach David "Dutch" Baer stands fourth from the left in the last row. During the 1920s and 1930s Baer served as director of the Playground Athletic League, which oversaw team sports at Easterwood Park. In that role he coached many if not all of the park's sports teams. The seven-acre West Baltimore green space lay on Baker Street between Moreland Avenue and Bentalou Street and became the neighborhood center for sports, club meetings, socializing, and teenage rites of passage.

pong room, a billiards room, a soda fountain, and a social hall were all in the basement.

Typically, as members were informed by the *Y Weekly* newsletter, the popular Rivers Chambers and his orchestra might be playing at a dance; at other times, the "Y Community Playhouse" might be staging a production like *Anna Christie.* On March 14, 1941, a "Giant Aquacade" was staged, "with Beautiful Girls, Singers, Water Ballet, Comedy Acts, Thrills," all in the Y pool. The same newsletter also noted: "The Cosmos Club defeated the Phoenix Club in basketball."

Armond Kessler belonged to the Y in the late 1930s. "Every Sunday morning the guys from Keyworth Avenue, all members of the Corsair Club, would go down to the Y and play basketball. The gym was always full and busy. They had leagues for every age and every level. We always played with the pick-up teams, any five guys playing any other five guys. I remember playing with Jack Pasarew, Bobby Orman, and Alleck Resnick. Best Sunday mornings in my life!"

When Charles Wagner was thirteen, he went to the Y every summer weekday on the Number 5 streetcar. He recalls, "I went at about ten o'clock in the morning carrying my lunch, which I ate in the cafeteria with a Coke I bought for a nickel. Though I took a class in building model airplanes, I spent most of my time taking lessons in lifesaving. I got good enough to become a lifeguard at Carlin's Park until 1944, when I went into the service. I have a lot to thank the old Y for."

Mynne Fox Shulman was active in the Y family from the 1930s through 1946. When she was twenty-seven, she recalled, "I was the youngest member of the Board of Directors. I was active in the Club Vivre, which for years was the Y's social dancing class program. We held weekly dances for servicemen stationed in the area. Lots of them must still remember those dancing classes, and maybe, just maybe, me as their teacher."

THE Y that my brother and I visited on those summer days in the early 1930s had grown out of the Jewish tradition that calls for the rich to help the poor—*tzedakah* at work.

Attempts to start a Jewish Y here as part of the national family of Jewish Y's can be traced as far back as 1854 and continued through the turn of the twentieth century. But for all of the communal interest, power, and money brought to bear to establish a Y in Baltimore, as late as 1917 there was little to show. In 1918 there was a historic breakthrough: On December 26 of that year, twenty young women met at the invitation of the Anna Sindler Literary Society at 1622 Madison Avenue, then the home of the Twentieth Century Athletic Club. Enthusiasm ran high and quickly translated into a plan of action. Workable plans for a "YW" were drawn up; the group committed to meeting regularly and working together until they had created a viable YWHA. The genie was out of the bottle.

Architect's rendering of the YM and YWHA planned for 305 West Monument Street. The Y opened in 1930, after several unsuccessful attempts to open a YM and YWHA in Baltimore. As a Jewish youth organization, the Y complemented the Jewish Educational Alliance (JEA), which began to serve the Jewish community in East Baltimore in 1910. Facilities at the new YM and YWHA included lounges, gym, clubrooms, health club, and, "suspended" on the second floor, a swimming pool with "seven large windows to bring in light." In the basement were the game room, soda fountain/cafeteria, and social hall.

By 1920, a regular schedule of activities, including drama, music, literature, and gym, was in place at "1622" (as the YW came to be known), at the homes of members, or, where called for, at other existing institutions.

The we-mean-business aspirations of the women energized the men. In August 1920, the men's group met at the Adelphi Clubroom at 2005 Madison Avenue and organized a Young Men's Hebrew Association. But unlike the women, who were content to operate without a permanent home, the men decided they would not open until they had one. The group set its sights on the building at 2005 Madison Avenue, but they could not raise the money.

It became clear that the YWHA and the YMHA had a joint mission—to secure a building that would house both organizations. Nevertheless, the women did not wait. When the opportunity presented itself in September 1921, the YW purchased the Twentieth Century Clubroom at 1622 Madison Avenue. Embarrassed, the men regrouped. In 1922 Harry Greenstein was elected president and led the YM to such strength and viability that it was able to buy the buildings at 2120-2126 Madison Avenue, at North Avenue, where it opened its facility in November 1923. The Baltimore Jewish community now had both a YMHA and YWHA, each operating in a different building.

As their programming called for more and more joint activities, it became clear to both the YMHA and the YWHA that their futures were bound together. They held joint dances, festivals, and High Holy Day observances; their publications treated both Ys as one. The arrangement seemed to work well—so well that in 1926 the women disposed of their building at 1622 Madison Avenue. The YMHA expanded to take in the house next to it, which was converted and fitted out as the "women's wing" of the Y. At long last, the men and the women were enjoying Y programming together in one building at North and Madison Avenues.

The obvious next step was to build a new and expanded YM and YWHA somewhere. To provide a rationale for fund-raising, the Jewish Welfare Board took a survey in 1925 to get a clear picture of what services existed for Jewish youth, and whether a new Y would result in overlapping of services. The survey results, made public on September 25, 1925, were more than enough to justify a combined YM and YWHA. The survey made clear that many Jewish boys and girls were using nonsectarian organizations instead of the synagogue centers, the JEA, or the Southwest Jewish Center. Of the 12,700 Jewish children of elementary school age, only 4,000 were receiving any Hebrew or religious education. Moreover, there were a worrisome

260 licensed poolrooms in Baltimore and a number of dance halls without proper supervision.

The study concluded by recommending that the YMHA and YWHA be merged and that money be raised for a building to house the combined organizations. The survey ignited community interest, and less than a year later, on May 27, 1926, the two were formally merged. In 1927 the Associated Jewish Charities bought the lot at 305 West Monument Street. The contract to build the new Y was given to Frainie Brothers and Haigley in November 1929 for $561,000 (exclusive of the cost of the land). The building was completed and opened to its members in July 1930 (a formal opening was held in October). Membership dues for children nine to thirteen were set at six dollars a year; for those fourteen and older the dues were nine dollars, including free laundry service for gym clothes.

The new building, spectacular for its day, was formally dedicated on October 19, 1930. The next morning, the *Sun* reported, "More than 2,000 members and their guests heard the congratulations of Governor Ritchie and Mayor Broening, overtaxing the capacity of the gymnasium auditorium and filling the lobby and the hallways.

"The exercises were opened with the presentation of the key to the new building by Aaron Straus, chairman of the building committee. Rabbi William Rosenau of the Eutaw Place Temple delivered the invocation; Rabbi Adolph Coblenz of Chizuk Amuno, the benediction."

The dedication continued with three plays by the Y Playshop. The program noted: "Tomorrow night, educational night, with Mrs. Florence Bamberger of Johns Hopkins University, presiding. Rabbi Solomon Goldman of Anshe Emet of Chicago will be principal speaker. A concert by the JEA orchestra will be heard on Wednesday night. Thursday, there will be exhibitions of boxing, wrestling, handball and swimming."

AT ABOUT 4:30 IN THE AFTERNOON on that August day in 1933, my brother Irving and I, refreshed by our swim and exhilarated by the enjoyment of a day's activities under the Y roof, called it a day. With wet bathing suits wrapped in our still-moist towels, we walked west to Druid Hill Avenue and caught the Number 5 streetcar, homeward bound, feeling very good that we had had another great day at the Monument Street Y.

All those who had worked long and hard to bring the Baltimore Y into being would be pleased with our sentiments.

Park Heights: The Street and the Life

Park Heights provided the ultimate northwest passage for Jews moving up the ladder, and out of East Baltimore.

Park Heights Avenue started out in the early twentieth century as a street and wound up as a way of life. Jews were drawn to Park Heights Avenue to live in its row houses, which were affordable, and its neighborhoods, which were hospitable—there were no "gentlemen's agreements" that kept Jews out; they also came to Park Heights Avenue to shop in its corner drug stores and its kosher butcher shops and to pray in its synagogues and temples. Many children of the Park Heights Avenue neighborhoods who are today grandfathers and grandmothers met their future spouses in Park Heights' street-corner society. On its backlot playing fields, young men met the mentors who would lead them into distinguished careers in medicine, law, and business.

Almost no one in Baltimore who is Jewish grew up without either living on or near Park Heights Avenue or visiting the street for one reason or another. The street has seen wars and depression and prosperity, as well as a paroxysm in its demographics. It has never stopped growing and changing. After three-quarters of a century, a new generation of people from around the world are bringing their own dreams to the avenue.

The halcyon days of Park Heights Avenue were the 1930s. Streetcars (Numbers 5 and 33) rumbled up and down its median strip, south to Park Circle and north to either West Arlington on Belvedere Avenue or to the "Manhattan Loop" on Park Heights, where a connecting bus served the "country" areas as far out as Glyndon. By the late 1930s the street had become distinctly Jewish, but well into the 1920s it remained mostly Protestant and Catholic. Meanwhile, before Lower Park Heights became a "changing" neighborhood in the 1950s, it had been one in the 1920s. During this first transition it had been the Protestants and Catholics in flight from the Jews.

Into the 1920s, Park Heights Avenue was a community of churches; there were only two synagogues: Shaarei Zion at 3459 and Shearith Israel at 5813. The massive St. Ambrose Catholic complex of church, school, and parish house was established at Park Heights and Wylie Avenues in 1907. The churches, like the synagogues, followed their congregants outward— Park Heights Avenue and Reisterstown Road to the west were becoming bedroom communities for people working downtown. Their move outward was made possible by the expansion of the streetcar lines serving the areas (Baltimore-Pimlico-Pikesville-Railroad); the streetcar lines themselves had gone into business largely in response to rider demand in the late 1870s created by the Maryland Jockey Club.

Pimlico provided streetcars with plenty of riders, going and coming. The Park Heights corridor leading north and west, unlike the streets leading north and east, was hospitable to Jews. "No Jews Allowed" signs never appeared on the lawns of homes for sale in the Park Heights corridor, and no signs of homes for sale on Park Heights contained the word "Restricted" (meaning, in the language of the day, "no Jews allowed"). The absence of such restrictions sent the right signals to Baltimore Jews concentrated in East Baltimore, Eutaw Place, and the streets intersecting West North Avenue, as they continued their northwest passage.

Park Delicatessen at 119 Park Avenue, in 1937. The store was owned and operated by William Abrahams and Philip Sabel. Jewish delis emerged out of East European immigrant culture as ethnic groceries. The signature sandwich generally was always a hot corned beef on rye with plenty of mustard and a pickle on the side.

UNTIL 1911 Park Heights Avenue was only 74 feet wide, but in that year, in response to increased traffic, the street was widened to 115 feet. "It will be a magnificent boulevard," the planners announced in a news account. "On each side there will be flower beds and shade trees, leaving the center open for vehicles and streetcar traffic." Indeed, a look at pictures of Park Heights Avenue in the 1930s shows that the planners made good on their promise. Employment of Jews in the retail, wholesale, and manufacturing businesses thriving downtown was growing, as was the Maryland Jockey Club, along with, as was pointed out earlier, the streetcar lines serving the neighborhoods.

Institutions followed. The Isaac Davidson Hebrew School opened in 1925, on Shirley Avenue between Park Heights and Reisterstown Road; Shearith Israel opened in its new building in 1925, at Glen Avenue and Park Heights Avenue; and Shaarei Zion opened in its new building in 1926, at 3459 Park Heights at Hilldale Avenue.

The Pimlico movie theater opened at 5132 Park Heights Avenue before America's involvement in World War I (1917) and continued to be a local favorite until it closed in 1952. The marquee here displays a hit from the 1938 season, Robert Donat and Rosalind Russell in *The Citadel*. (Courtesy of Robert Headley.)

Onto the drawing board went the Park Heights neighborhoods that would become the stuff of nostalgia to a generation that grew up in them from about 1915 through the 1950s: Ulman, Hilldale, Violet, Keyworth, and Shirley Avenues and all the other streets intersecting Park Heights all the way from Park Circle to Pimlico. Then the "Upper Park Heights" neighborhoods: Fords Lane, Taney Road, and Pinkney Road up to Slade Avenue. But it was the row house neighborhoods below Belvedere that would prove the biggest and most powerful magnet drawing people to the Park Heights corridor.

The typical price for a row house in the 1920s ranged from two thousand to seven thousand dollars—considered a good value even in those days. The Jews who moved into these row houses were middle class: compared to the city as a whole, they were well educated, with most having at least an eighth-grade education. The move out for them was a move from crowded, over-the-store rooms on teeming streets of commerce to an airy house on a clean, hedge-lined suburban vista.

Advertising beckoned these prospective residents. An ad for the area from Park Circle to Spring Hill Avenue, called Cottage Hill (taking in Cottage Avenue) read, "The neighborhood will withstand any economic change and will increase in value. The location is unique. Beautiful terraced fronts. Spacious rears with yard, with large trees as background, an atmosphere of hills within one block of transportation. Only 20 minutes to Howard and Lexington."

A generation coming of age since World War II that grew up on and near Park Heights Avenue can recall its elementary schools (P.S. 59, Louisa May Alcott; P.S. 223, Pimlico; and P.S. 234, Arlington); its corner drug stores (Sussman's, Hillman's, Sidlen's, Lewis's, Zentz's, Beeli's); its delis (Lapides at Park Circle, Kessler's, Cooper's); its *cheders*, *shochets*, and synagogues. By the 1960s many of the established congregations, including the recently formed Beth El, and all of the Eutaw Place Reform congregations—Har Sinai, Oheb Shalom, and Baltimore Hebrew ("Rabbi Morris Lieberman's congregation")—had moved out to Park Heights Avenue .

And so had many families, some of whom would go on to prominence—the Joseph Meyerhoffs, for example. Harvey "Bud" Meyerhoff, Joseph's son, writing in his memoirs, notes, "When I was a young boy we lived in Upper Park Heights, Pinkney Road in particular. In 1940 and 1941 Dad built another, larger house in a more upscale area, Fallstaff. Both of those neighborhoods, along with others in the Park Heights corridor, were wholly Jewish, or nearly so."

Harvey's grandparents (Oscar and Hannah) came to America as impoverished immigrants from, according to Mr. Meyerhoff, Pereschipina in the Ukraine in 1906, when their son, Joseph, was seven. In time, Oscar and Hannah went into the grocery and kosher meat business, and Oscar also became a part-time cantor. Joseph Meyerhoff attended the accelerated P.S. 49 (directly across Cathedral Street from what, seven decades later, would be the site of the symphony hall bearing his name) and then went on to earn a law degree. The Meyerhoff family went on to become renowned real estate developers with a world-wide reputation for philanthropy.

The "golden age" of Park Heights Avenue that began in the 1920s was central to Baltimore Jewish life and lasted through the end of World War II and a few years beyond. The Jewish neighborhoods that formed in Park Heights during the 1920s began to break up in the 1950s with a speed that matched the changes in American life in general and Jewish life in postwar America in particular. The Associated Jewish Charities joined the movement "out of Park Heights." The Jewish Community Center, Baltimore Hebrew College, Jewish Family Services—all materialized on Upper Park Heights Avenue.

The 1960s were the pivotal years in the history of Park Heights Avenue. In the fifty years between the mid-1940s and the mid-1990s, Lower Park Heights went into a fit of change. The opening of the suburbs, driven by easy money, vehicular access, and new schools energized the movements of many whites, Jewish and gentile, out of Park Heights and into the suburbs. The whole stretch of Park Heights, from Park Circle to Pimlico and out to the city line, once almost entirely Jewish, became, by the 1960s, largely African American. That situation is changing once again today. Upper Park Heights has taken on still another life, as the Orthodox community moves into these neighborhoods, reinvigorating the very same blocks abandoned by Jews in earlier years.

In 1911 the *Sun* had occasion to reference Park Heights Avenue: "The drive is popular," it observed, "because it leads to the suburbs." A curiously prescient observation.

The Jewish Deli: A Place to Meet and Eat

The delis are to the Jews of Northwest Baltimore what taverns are to residents of Highlandtown—a place to eat, yes, but also a place to meet, to greet, to enjoy comfort food in the company of old friends. The haunting aroma of warm rye bread, hot corned beef, sizzling pastrami, mustard, and pickle-barrel brine that wafts through delis links father to son, friend to friend, the present with the past.

The most popular of the many delis that once dotted the northwest section of Baltimore was undoubtedly Nates and Leon's. The legendary deli traced its origins to 1937, when Nathan Herr and his friend Leon Shaivitz, with limited experience in the business, opened a deli at North and Linden Avenues. But they knew this much about running a restaurant: if you build great sandwiches, they will come. That is the Nates and Leon's story: They built their sandwiches big, and doctors and lawyers and business tycoons, along with strippers and racetrack touts and numbers runners, flocked to the place twenty-four hours a day.

Nates Herr used to say, "The people and the hours—we were open twenty-four hours a day—helped make us popular, but so did the food." He was talking about their "Number Three": corned beef, Russian dressing, and cole slaw. "No way to beat it," he would say. The credit for the deli's fame belonged to Nates and Leon's overwhelming sandwiches—chicken salad, turkey, tongue, brisket, and pastrami—all in dizzying combinations, or, perhaps, to their mountainous pastries, strawberry short cake, Napoleons, and chocolate eclairs. When the old place went on the auction block in 1967—tables, chairs, crockery, cutlery, counters, the works—auctioneer Leon Zalis opened the bids. To the crowd assembled at this sad funeral, he pleaded, "Ladies and gentlemen, hold back your tears."

Ballow's, at 2115 West North Avenue, gave the world what it now takes for granted: the formidable hot dog-bologna combination. In this creation, grease from the bologna mixes with the grease from the hot dog, and the combined mix finds its way into the roll to form an unforgettable aroma, taste, and aftertaste, while adding maybe two hundred points to one's cholesterol count. When you eat the combo today, eat it in memory of Nathan Ballow. In 1956 Ballow's became Mandell-Ballow in the Hilltop Shopping Center at Reisterstown Road at Rogers Avenue.

Sussman and Lev's was probably the first full-scale delicatessen restaurant in Baltimore. And one of the longest lived. Founded in 1922 as Sussman's at 923 East Baltimore Street, the smallish neighborhood deli continually expanded and began to attract people from all over town. The number and variety of their sandwiches were legendary. An early menu offered lox and cream cheese, spiced beef, corned beef, roast beef, salami, chopped liver, and an invitation to wash it all down with an Almond Smash soda. Sussman and Lev drew a standing-room-only lunch crowd from the industrial plants that once flourished in East Baltimore. Those plants disappeared in the 1950s, and so did Sussman and Lev's.

The aroma of hot corned beef and mustard on warm rye bread links father to son, the past with the present.

An exception to the all but mandatory Northwest Baltimore location for a Jewish deli was Awrach and Perl, on Howard Street between Lexington and Saratoga Streets in the heart of the downtown retail district. On any given Saturday morning in the 1930s and 1940s, you were lucky to get in. Their menu, of which H. L. Mencken was said to be a devotee, offered sixteen omelets, forty-seven sandwiches, and generous servings of chopped liver. Hilda Perl Goodwin reminisced that in its glory days, before it closed in 1944, Awrach and Perl was reportedly "the largest buyer of hot dogs in Baltimore."

Attman's of Lombard Street still survives, thanks to the gods who must dearly love old delis. The place is as it used to be in the 1930s: the corned beef on the slicer, the pickle in the brine, the homemade signs hand-scrawled and slapped in wild disorder on the walls.

In memory of all the delis that have come and gone, one should find a good deli (there are always plenty of them out there, they come and they go) and enjoy. Order up a heartburn on rye.

And don't hold the mustard.

Isaac Davidson: The Man, the School, the Memories

Baltimore's first Jewish school built solely as a Hebrew school.

Isaac Davidson Hebrew School was unique not only because it was the first school to be built solely as a Hebrew school but also because it offered a curriculum that combined play with work, as the old *cheders* did not. It was a combination that worked well; the school's graduates tell you they are bonded in a separate society. Many became leaders in the academic (Jewish and secular), business, and professional communities. Each, in reflection and reminiscence, attributes much of his or her success in life to the enduring influence of Isaac Davidson Hebrew School. Gathering at Baltimore Hebrew College on the night of February 4, 1951, to mark the twenty-fifth anniversary of the founding of Isaac Davidson Hebrew School (the school opened its doors October 4, 1925) celebrants outdid one another in their extravagant praise for the school and its alumni.

Speaker after speaker (including Dr. Louis L. Kaplan, Isaac Potts, and M. Henry Kuntz) elaborated on the message set out in the printed program by the school's longtime principal, Dr. Sidney I. Esterson: "Graduates of Isaac Davidson have served, and still serve, as Hebrew teachers imparting to hundreds of children the inspiration of a good Jewish education such as they acquired at Isaac Davidson. They are in the forefront of all local Jewish youth movements such as Young Judea and Habonim."

Ringing applause greeted each claim for the school's influence, distinction, importance. But had one read the story of the school's formation as it was recorded in the Baltimore *Jewish Times* of October 1924, one would not have predicted an evening of such self-congratulation:

> About a year ago, the Hebrew Education Society, realizing more than the very inhabitants themselves that the Park Heights section was in dire need of a modern Hebrew school for modern instruction, began to build one. It was then that the Jews of this section, numerous as they are, began to show their ungratefulness. They evinced very little interest in the project which meant so much to them and gave it very little support.
>
> Has this beautiful and imposing building aroused the Park Heights Jews from their torpor of indifference? Hardly. Just as they were slow to aid in the erection of the building, so are they slow to take advantage of the completed building. The school has been open for more than three weeks for registration and out of a possible 700 or 800 children from this section, a bare 90 have been registered.
>
> What is the reason for the indifference of the Park Heights Jews to their new Hebrew school? It is sincerely to be hoped that registration in the next few weeks will be so great as to remove all these doubts.

That was three quarters of a century ago. History rewarded the hope of the forlorn *Jewish Times* writer who viewed with such despair the unpromising beginning of Isaac Davidson. The school and its life, its soaring times, and the intense nostalgia it evokes among alumni are now bright chapters in the history of the Baltimore Jewish community.

Mr. Isaac Davidson, after whom the school was named, was a prominent German-born businessman who took an interest in the affairs of the East European Jews. As was typical for young men of his class, he was educated privately in the best schools in Europe. He came to New York in 1869 to clerk for his uncles. Shortly thereafter, he went to Alabama on a business venture, then in 1884 he came to Baltimore to start a furniture business. His father was a cantor who came from a long line of cantors, and this deep background in Judaism apparently drew Mr. Davidson to Jewish affairs.

For reasons of ill health, Isaac Davidson resigned his position as president of the Baltimore Hebrew College on March 13, 1925; by then the Isaac

Davidson Hebrew School project was well under way and the school would open that October. Mr. Davidson died that year, but we do not know when, nor whether he was present at the opening ceremony. The records do not make entirely clear why the school was named for Mr. Davidson.

According to Thomas Lipnick, a director of the Baltimore Hebrew College at the time of the twenty-fifth anniversary celebration of the Isaac Davidson Hebrew School and an active supporter of Jewish education in Baltimore, Isaac Davidson Hebrew School developed out of the Hebrew Education Society. The society was founded in 1860 and was the first Jewish educational institution in Baltimore, preceding the Hebrew Free School by twenty-nine years.

The society's first known location was at 125 Aisquith Street. In 1913, responding to growth and change in Jewish neighborhoods, the society opened a branch at 106 Jackson Place. The Aisquith Street building was converted into a training school for Hebrew teachers, which six years later became the Baltimore Hebrew College. In 1920 the society merged its schools and opened a new, larger facility at Baltimore and Chester Streets, which became known as the Ezra Hebrew School.

At that time, Baltimore had six independent Hebrew schools, known as the Talmud Torahs, the generic name for Jewish community schools. When one of them, Baltimore Talmud Torah, moved from the 1000 block of East Baltimore Street further out, east, to spacious, new quarters on Broadway, the directors of the Hebrew Education Society decided to move the Ezra Hebrew School further out, northwest, where Jews were moving in considerable numbers. A site on Shirley Avenue, between Park Heights Avenue and Reisterstown Road, was chosen, and the new school, its name changed to Isaac Davidson Hebrew School, opened to pupils in 1925.

The first graduating class was the class of 1930: Rena Sharp, Herbert Klein, Elsie Shpritz, Emanuel Katz, Ada Sauber, and Leonard Woolf.

Nearly thirty years after its closing, Isaac Davidson School's teachings and memories are still in the minds of many. Leonard Woolf entered Isaac Davidson Hebrew School in 1925, when he was nine years old, and attended through his Bar Mitzvah and one year beyond. "Dr. (Sidney) Esterson had a most interesting way of preparing his students for Bar Mitzvah," Mr. Woolf recalls. "He used the mentor system. Older boys would teach the younger boys. In my case, an older student, Harry Korsover, taught me my Haftorah."

Mr. Woolf continues:

Jewish boys who attended Isaac Davidson retain strong memories of the experience. First, the curriculum allowed the students, and the school encouraged them, to play softball. We used to travel to Patterson Park and Carroll Park, to play the other Talmud Torah schools. Once, we were in Carroll Park to play the Southwest Talmud Torah students, and our coach saw that we were going to win. He said, "Boys, these Southwest guys are tough. When you see the last out, pick up your glove and get the hell out!" We did, too.

The school grew to be a neighborhood center where young people could meet. There were clubs, like the Young Judea. And for a time the building actually became the uptown branch of the old East Baltimore JEA and home to even more clubs and activities.

Royal Parker (Pollokoff) entered Isaac Davidson in 1935 when he was six years old. "I was there on a special deal, a dollar a month. Others who could afford it paid five dollars a month. I went every day except Friday and Saturday," he says.

Shoe repair shop of Jacob Ellenson (*right*) at 3457 Chestnut Avenue in Hampden.

Dr. Sidney Esterson ran the place with a firm but friendly hand: he was always disciplining. He'd keep you after school, or have you sit in his office, or write sentences over and over, the usual punishments for elementary school kids. My favorite teachers were Mr. Tchack and Mr. Weinstein and Mrs. Sadowsky, who taught me my Haftorah. And looking back, part of the genius of the Baltimore Hebrew School experience: we played a lot of softball at Isaac Davidson. By the way, Dr. Esterson played softball with us. So did Dr. Kaplan.

Going to Isaac Davidson opened the world up to me, at least the world of Northwest Baltimore. Today, when I drive down Park Heights Avenue, my sons all get ready for my grand tour. They know that the highlights of that tour are my memories of Isaac Davidson Hebrew School. The building is still there. And sometimes I think I am too.

Edwin "Eddie" Snyder presents anyone who asks him about Isaac Davidson with his diploma, which he earned when he was fifteen in 1937. He remembers in particular the speakers who came from what was then Palestine; they presented huge maps and talked about Zionism and about rebuilding the land to become "some day" a homeland for the Jewish people. "Israel was not founded until 1948," Mr. Snyder said, "but in Isaac Davidson we were preparing for it in 1936."

Muriel Woolf Kramer entered Isaac Davidson in 1932, when she was nine years old, and graduated when she was thirteen.

The students were mostly boys and it seemed to us girls that they played an awful lot of softball. And when they did, there wasn't much else for us to do but watch them. Which is what we did.

The school provided an opportunity to meet boys and girls your own age, not in just the school itself but in the Young Judea club and in the clubs of the Northwest JEA, for a time housed in the same building. I not only met friends there that I kept for life, I developed an attachment for Judaism that has been important to me down to today.

We loved Mr. Tchack, he was certainly my favorite teacher. He got us reading books and speaking Hebrew very early, and it seems to me he did it in the gentlest of manners. We liked him so much we visited him at home. He lived on Shirley Avenue. And years after, when he was sick long after Isaac Davidson had closed, we visited him in the hospital. It comforted him, I am sure, to see his old students come home to him.

Sarajane Gold Greenfeld started at Isaac Davidson in 1938, when she was six years old.

My sister Trina and I were among the very few students there who were not attending either P.S. 59 or 18. We lived just north of Cold Spring Lane on Oakford Avenue so we went to Pimlico Elementary. We were sort of outsiders for a while.

We studied *chumash*, Hebrew, grammar, and history under great teachers, like Elsie Shpritz Berger, Rose Becker, Kopel Weinstein, Harry Tchack. The curriculum was intense. When I was a student at Isaac Davidson I had read seventeen novels in Hebrew, including *Oliver Twist* and *King Solomon's Mines*.

The school had a formula that somehow worked to make kids like the place. Maybe it was because they knew just how much picnicking and softball and plays to mix in with the studying. I remember we used to march down to Druid Hill Park on Lag b'Omer and have mock battles with bows and arrows like the kids in Israel. My sister Trina won the Queen Esther contest twice, which meant that I could never win it even once! It would have looked fixed for the Gold sisters.

Isaac Davidson is still very much with me. Wherever I go I meet former classmates. We are always so glad to see each other. There is a special bond between us. It will always be there.

Harry London started at Isaac Davidson in 1929. "Sentences! Sentences were the punishment of choice at Isaac Davidson!" he remembers. "I wrote hundreds of sentences. 'I will not throw spitballs, I will not throw spitballs, I will not throw spitballs.'" London continues, "A significant number of graduates became rabbis, encouraged by Dr. Kaplan. Among them, Jerry and Bernie Lipnick, Herman and Philip Kieval and Jerry Grollman."

In the early 1960s, a profound change was taking place in the Park Heights Avenue corridor. History would call it, in its simplest terms, "white flight." The Jewish community was part of this flight, and when it abandoned its neighborhoods it abandoned the institutions that served them, including the Isaac Davidson Hebrew School.

Rabbi Herbert Birnbaum was principal of the school at that time, having arrived in 1957. "Here we were," he recalls, "on Park Heights Avenue, a school that at one time had six hundred students, had, in the early 1960s, less than sixty. This, in a school that once had its children attending classes Sunday through Thursday, then coming back for shabbos services on Saturday." Rabbi Birnbaum goes on:

But in the early 1960s, reality set in. How could we reach the Jewish children when there were so few of them in our classrooms? The Board of Jewish Education took cognizance, and in 1962 closed the school on Shirley Avenue, and sold it that same year to the Baltimore City School System, which used the building as an annex to P.S. 59 just across the street. The students were transferred to the Petach Tikvah school on Denmore Avenue. The school then took a hyphenated name: "Petach Tikvah-Isaac Davidson." I was not too sorry to see it all happen. I felt that as long as we could educate our children, I was satisfied.

In 1967 Petach Tikvah closed. It was over.

And the Isaac Davidson Hebrew School became one with history.

Summer Camps: An Extension of Jewish Family and Social Circle

The choice was a statement by your family of who you, and they, were.

If in the 1930s and 1940s you were eight to sixteen years old, you may have been at Baltimore's Penn Station on June 27 of any one of those years, part of a crowd of camp-bound children. Some were accompanied by adults, some were singing, some were crying. It was the one day each year when hundreds of children of Jewish families, most of whom lived in the Lake Drive, Park Heights, Forest Park, and Mount Washington neighborhoods, waited for the Montrealer, the Pennsylvania Railroad train that would take them to New York or Boston. There they would switch to a bus or another train, disembarking at camps scattered all over New York and New England. This festival of departure was for children who were "going north," though far more went to camps that were closer, if less prestigious.

The "summer camp" chapter in the history of the Jewish community (and the non-Jewish, too, for that matter) was about getting out of the city and into the woods, about parents' fear of polio back when it was believed that the dreaded disease struck in crowded cities, and about a family's perception of where in the communal social order it thought it belonged—or wanted to belong. Where you went to summer camp as a child communicated who you were, how you lived, who your friends were. The choice of a summer camp was a fairly reliable imprint of a family's lifestyle, real or desired.

Nelson Hyman was one of hundreds of young Baltimore men who, over the years, went to Camp Hawaya in Harrison, Maine. He went every summer from 1946 to 1954. He looks back at that time of his life:

There were a lot of Jewish kids living in the Lake Drive area, and Dave Kaufman, a very popular teacher at City College and the owner of Hawaya, lived on the corner of Brookfield and Brooks Lane, in that same neighborhood. Quite naturally, he knew a lot of the families in that neighborhood and they knew him, and his camp. Though I lived in Fairmount, Walbrook Junction and Windsor Hills, I had a lot of friends over in the Eutaw Place–Brookfield Avenue neighborhood and my parents knew Dave. I was also close to a great group of City College guys going to Hawaya—Bobby Hammerman, Jerry Sachs, Benson Offit, Sid Offit, Erv Sekulow. I joined the crowd.

Betty Max Wise went to Camp Owaissa in Massachusetts. She adds to the legend of "Camp Day" in Baltimore that began in the morning, in her case at Mount Royal Station:

Those of us going to New York and Massachusetts met at New York's Grand Central Station, which on the day we were leaving seemed to have been taken over by Jewish kids going to camps. Each camp's group would get together in some corner of the station and raise a placard with the camp's name on it, and sing the camp song. It was exciting, like some kind of festival, at least for the kids who wanted to go and weren't crying.

When the camp train came in, you could see in a window of each car a big, colorful placard that designated that car for a particular camp. I remember the cheering and the chanting! Owaissa was the girls' camp. The boys' camp was Monterey.

Phillip Macht left Penn Station every year for eleven years (1934 to 1944) to go to Camp Cody. The camp was located first in Little Meadows, Pennsylvania, and later moved to Lake Ossipee, New Hampshire. "I loved the place," Mr. Macht says. "Every year I looked forward to meeting campers from other cities. Remember, these were the days before air conditioning, and the New England woods were not so bad a place for young boys to cavort. At Cody I was good at everything, and not very good at anything. My counselors were Merle Debuskey, Morty Benesch, and Nate Schnaper. My contemporaries were Morty Land and Albert Aaron."

Irving Lansman worked at Camp Cody as a waiter in the summer of 1939. "Phil Axman, who owned the camp, chose six of us from City College for the job. Along with me were Al Nathanson and Alvin Rudo. Sid Lipsch was in charge of the camp and Charley Rudo was head counselor. It was a beautiful camp, and we didn't work very hard."

Many Baltimore parents sent their children to camp in the country out of fear of a polio epidemic breaking out in the city. Ironically, in 1944—a year some people will never forget—a polio epidemic broke out in the camps themselves. That year, Murray Miller was a camper at Camp Idylwold, on Schroon Lake, in New York. Murray recalls: "Late in that August a number of campers suddenly became very ill. They were rushed to a hospital in a town on Lake George and were diagnosed as having polio. Among

Abraham's Tobacco and Candy Shop at 1006 West Baltimore Street, ca. 1932. Abraham Cherney, *right*; Sylvan Cherney, *left*.

those stricken were Lee Bacharach, Morris Wolf, and Bobby Hess. Word went around like wildfire. We were quickly packed and sent home on the next day. Parents met us at Penn Station. It was a sad homecoming.

"Interesting thing about Camp Idylwold," Murray Miller continues, focusing on better years there, "it was generally true that the Jewish camps were made up of the kids from either East European or German Jewish families. But at Idylwold, the groups came together."

Robert Ginsburg went to Camp Kennebec in Maine. "Every summer from 1949 to 1956, I joined Leonard Goodman, Phil Wetzler, Bobby Millhauser, John Haas, Stuart Rome, George Hess, Harry Blum, Herb Katzenberg and a lot of guys from the Suburban Club. We all left Penn Station late in June for eight blissful weeks," Mr. Ginsburg says. "The highlight of those years was a two-week canoe trip up the Allagash River, into the north woods. You don't forget those days and nights."

Kalman "Buzzy" Hettleman went to Camp Wigwam in Maine from 1944 to 1950. "Some kids went there as long as twelve years," he says:

Mark Joseph went from the time he was six. Wigwam became a large part of our lives, the friendships, the spirit, the camaraderie. Maybe other camps left their alumni and alumnae with this same legacy of fondness and remembrance, like ties to an old neighborhood. I don't know. I know it's true of Wigwam.

There seemed to be a mix of Jews from both German Jewish families and Russian Jewish. Wigwam campers included Morton Blaustein and Bobby Goodman, and curiously, the children of scrap metal dealers from around the country, from Detroit and Cleveland and throughout Pennsylvania, a group which took in my cousin Michael, "Sonny" Plant, and me.

J. D. Salinger went there. So did Frank Loesser, the songwriter and producer of *Guys and Dolls*, and Richard Rodgers of Rodgers and Hammerstein. Camp folklore had it that "Surrey with a Fringe on Top" came from a Camp Wigwam show.

Joan Green Klein went to Camp Somerset in Maine from 1943 to 1947. "It's true that many of the girls from the German Jewish families went to Tripp Lake and Tapawingo, but I never gave it much thought," she says. Mrs. Klein continues:

We went up on the train and stayed overnight in Boston. Looking back, we were not always ideal campers. One year we threw eggs out of our hotel window and were understandably regarded as a bunch of rude kids. I was with Ruth Glick Cohen, Sarah Offit Abeshouse, Barbara Wolfsheimer Taylor, Barbara Katz Judd, Myra Levenson Askin, Ellen Sachs Fedder, Judy Carliner Rosenberg.

Somerset was different from many Maine camps. Our bunks were rustic. We had no dances, no social life. The emphasis was on week-long canoe trips on the Belgrade Lakes and the Kennebec River, and we portaged those canoes, too!

Mrs. Klein's sister-in-law, Betty Mae Klein Gelfand, went to Camp Tapawingo in Maine. "I went from 1941 to 1943, with my friends from the German Jewish families I knew at Park School, Helen Mary Benesch Strauss, Bobby Gutman, Lorraine Lazarus. It was a very old camp. Ellen Zamoiski's *mother* went there! It's where I learned to smoke, right behind the bunk." Her brother Joe went to Camp Belgrade with Richard Eliasberg, Irvin Greif, and Richard Schleisner.

Malcolm Mahr was the camper of campers: he went to Camp Cody (1941 to 1945), Camp Wigwam (1946 to 1950), and Camp Skylemar in Maine (1951 to 1955). Mahr attended Skylemar because he was considered a star basketball player and Skylemar was "a camp for athletics." "Most all of the staff were athletic directors or coaches," Malcolm recalls. "I was there with guys from both Woodholme and Suburban. Jimmy Tuvin, Jay Blumenthal, Stuart Blankman. No matter how good or bad at athletics you were when you came to Skylemar, when you left you were a whole lot better."

By far, however, most of the children of Baltimore's Jewish families in those years did not go to New York or New England. They went to camps nearby. Many went to Camp Airy and Camp Louise, an hour away in Thurmont, Maryland. Sidney Chernak, who managed Airy and Louise, estimates that in those years, as many as fifteen hundred children went to those two camps each summer. Lois Schenker Madow went to Wohelo, a girls' camp in Waynesboro, Pennsylvania. "It was in between. It wasn't Maine, and it wasn't Louise," she says. "We had indoor plumbing, but only cold water. We didn't take canoe trips, but we did take long hikes. In my gang were Gerry Oberfeld Feinglass, Debbie Kronthal Ring, Molly Lesnick Bereson. I went there eight summers—eight summers without seeing a boy!"

Many others went to Camp Habonim. In 1952, Barbara Milgrome Cohen was one of them, heading for Riva, near Annapolis, and a different kind of coed summer camp. She recalls: "The camp, in Hebrew, meant 'the builders' and it was modeled after the Israeli *kibbutzim*, and the children were from Zionist families. We did all the work. Cooking, cleaning, building the cabins we slept in. We spoke Hebrew, we studied Jewish history, we kept Shabbos. The camp housed about a hundred kids. Among them, Jay Fisher, Frank Schoenfeld, Annie Mauer, Helen Bronstein and Ben Bronstein. The experience gave us a sense of Jewish identity for a lifetime."

Edwin "Eddy" Snyder and his three brothers went to Camp Airy for the entire summer each year from 1928 to 1932, when, he recalls, it cost ten dollars a week. "My brother Nathan was a medical student and worked in the dispensary. Aaron was a counselor, Milton was a waiter. But my parents had to pay for me. On Saturday night we had boxing matches. My brothers kept putting me in them and I kept getting killed. But on Friday nights we went over to Camp Louise and things were gentler. The girls put on plays."

Doris Schwartz Malin was one of the girls in the plays at Camp Louise. "I went to Louise, off and on, over a ten-year period, 1944 to 1955," she recounts. "I will always remember Aunt Lillie and Uncle Airy. They lived in a cottage in the camp. Every day on our way to the lake they would wave to us. Louise attracted campers from around the country, including Ann Landers' daughter, from Wisconsin. I still see my old campmates Carole Sibel, Nan Rosenthal, and Nikki Fortunato."

Adults reminiscing about their summer camp experience of those days become sentimental. They talk about a rite of passage, a childhood of bonding, about reunions and summers long ago. Lifelong friendships grew out of those relationships; so did marriages.

There were dozens of camps popular among Jewish families in those days, though there is room here to name only some. They were for the rich and the poor; for the German Jews and Russian Jews; they were nearby and far away. Some camps were mixes of all of these characteristics. But in the end, the camp where one wound up was usually an extension of one's family, social circle, and home.

P.S. 49: The Jewish "Private School"

The year was 1940. At P.S. 49, at 1205 Cathedral Street, across from where the Meyerhoff is today, a teacher posed this question to her class of seventh graders: "We have been discussing the characteristics of great men, and why we admire them. Will the class suggest some great women whom we may admire?" In response to the teacher's question, many hands shot up and a flood of names poured forth: Clara Barton, Florence Nightingale, Eleanor Roosevelt, Dolly Madison. After a brief pause, a boy shouted, "Marie Antoinette!" The class burst into derisive laughter. Then, the boy who had mentioned France's ill-starred queen rose courageously to defend his answer.

"She was an Austrian duchess," he said. "She came to France, which was very strange to her, and she married a French king who neglected her. She did not love him. But she did love to be humble. That is why she had a cottage in Petit Trianon, and used to imagine herself a simple milkmaid. Later, they cut off her head." An answer you might expect. Except that the boy was eleven years old.

"Forty-Nine," as it was affectionately known, is unique in Jewish communal memory, owing its special place to its academic excellence. Because of that reputation, many Jewish families, traditionally viewing education as a high priority, sought to have their children attend. The aspiration was not misplaced: nearly every student at P.S. 49 had an I.Q. of 110 or better, and all but a few were considerably above that, some going as high as 140. The average at P.S. 49 was 135 in the 1940s, a time when the average "intelligence rating" for all junior high schools in Baltimore was 107.

Alumnus Sander Wise recalls, "When I went there in the early 1940s the Jewish population of Baltimore may have been, say, 3 percent. But in my class, at least 30 percent of the class was Jewish. Among them, Betty Max (the future Mrs. Sander Wise), Thalia Dragon, Malcolm Jaffee, and Daniel Glick." Bennard Perlman went to P.S. 49 in 1940 and 1942. He remembers:

We had the greatest teachers! Margery Harriss taught English. Madame Calvert, French. Dena Cohen, music. Helen Cohen, history. Zilla Benesch was my art teacher and was responsible for my career in art. It was she who led me to take the special new art curriculum being offered at City College and sponsored by the Carnegie Foundation. She, and Forty-Nine, gave me new purpose and direction, and changed my life.

Physically, the building and its limited facilities kept us, by today's standards, deprived. There were three floors in this tiny building on Cathedral Street. A small gym was directly behind, facing Maryland Avenue. There was a little courtyard in between.

Margery Harriss taught English from 1941 to 1951. Reminiscing about Forty Nine, Mrs. Harriss bubbled with joy:

Some thought of P.S. 49 as the Jews' very own "private" school.

We had such bright children! You had to be invited to go to Forty-Nine, you know. I taught *Ivanhoe*, *Silas Marner*, *Rime of the Ancient Mariner*, *Julius Caesar*, and *Macbeth*. When we studied a Shakespeare play, I asked the students to think of themselves in the Globe Theater watching the original Shakespeare, and I tried to arrange the seating to resemble the Globe's.

When I think back, the level of discussion was remarkable, but I shouldn't have been surprised. My classes included children like Elaine Isaacson Katzen, Liebe Sokol, Herbert Wagner, Jackie Cohen Brodie, Diane Krostar, Jonathan and Manfred Guttmacher, Stephen Sachs.

Most kids had to walk over to School 79 to take home economics or shop, all the way to Park Avenue and Hoffman Street, and some of the streets they had to cross were heavily trafficked. Baltimore City was progressive in establishing an accelerated school like Forty Nine, but they might have worked out a less dangerous arrangement than that walk. Nobody ever got hurt. Amazing.

One of Mrs. Harriss' Shakespeare students was Sue Levin Hess. "I started quoting Shakespeare in Mrs. Harriss' class, and fell in love with theater, right then and there. Theater arts became a part of my life and they are down to this day. My first love was a boy in my class, Lewis Kann."

The school's reputation for having a high percentage of Jewish students is reinforced by a 1930 graduate, writing in a 1986 reunion program, "The school was about half Jewish. Although I am a gentile, I came to admire the Jewish people. At Forty Nine, although they were probably no more intelligent than the gentiles, they were more industrious and highly motivated."

Formally named the Robert E. Lee School, P.S. 49 was a no-nonsense, all-academic prep school, unashamed of its intellectual elitism. There were only about 400 students, no auditorium and no labs, although there was a small gym. (A study of the students at the time concluded: "These students are not particularly interested in exercise.") The curriculum called for students' completing three years work in two; each student was expected to do three hours of homework every night.

The school's architecture, according to a prominent realtor operating in the area, was "one of the greats of this neighborhood, with generous amounts of carved brownstone and terracotta work." In 1977, fifteen years after the school shut down, the building was renovated for the expansion of the Medical and Chirurgical Faculty of the State of Maryland, located next door.

Among the hundreds attending that 1986 Reunion were Hilda Fivel Goodwin, Ira Askin, Ruth Surosky Levy, Ruth Wolpert Rudick, Gerald Jeffein, Joseph Pines, Sarajane Gold Greenfeld, Ann Hettleman Kahan, Frederika Kolker Saxon, Kalman Hettleman, Beverly Max Penn, Bonnie Fox London, Mary Perl Azrael, Herbert Katzenberg, Lucille Blumenthal Karr, Donald Kann, Stuart Fine, Lester Ellin, Babette Hecht Rosenberg, S. Leonard Sollins, M. Sigmund Shapiro, Mildred Mashkes Dubois, Carol Chaimson Sibel, and Shirley Berman Patt.

FOLLOWING THE DISCUSSION of great women, the teacher asked the class to say the Pledge of Allegiance to the flag. Which they did. In Latin.

The school opened in 1909 and closed on a sad day in June 1962. On that day, the students heard, for the last time ever in "Forty Nine," the pedagogical imperative, "Class dismissed!"

Forest Park: The Alternative to Park Heights

To you Forest Park we are loyal
To you we will always be true
And our love will survive, for we
always will strive
To keep it alive, Forest Park

Forest Park came into being as a Jewish neighborhood in the 1920s because it lay in the path of the Jewish community's northwest passage.

These were the years when families of East European descent began to enjoy the economic fruits of their hard labors. Living in the row house neighborhoods of South, West, and East Baltimore, they were looking to trade concrete for greenery and to gain the feeling of moving up by moving "out." In this northwesterly move, the dynamics of Baltimore's Jewish social structure presented the Jewish middle class, mostly the Jews of Eastern European origins, with a choice: "Upper" Park Heights (above Rogers Avenue) or Forest Park. Thousands chose Forest Park.

Joseph Kaufman, who lived in Forest Park most of his life, theorized that Forest Park was the choice of so many because, first, "the houses in general cost less. Second, the grass was as green in Forest Park as it was in Upper Park Heights. But third, and maybe the most persuasive reason, in Forest Park there were a lot of cost-friendly duplexes."

"When we first moved to Forest Park, we lived in the 3400 block of Fairview Avenue," he recalled. "It was the second floor of a duplex. Rent from our tenant downstairs, Dr. David Tenner, made it possible for us to buy the house. Later, we moved to a detached house at 3512 Springdale Avenue. Forest Park's duplexes, that brought in money against the mortgage, were its secret weapon in competition with Upper Park Heights."

More than the enticing economics of duplex rental, what enhanced Forest Park's image was the presence of Rabbi Samuel Rosenblatt and the institution he headed, Beth Tfiloh Synagogue. The neighborhood, the shul, and its charismatic leader (he spoke nine languages, wrote ten books, and taught at Johns Hopkins University) were bound together for almost half a century, from 1921 to 1966.

Almost no one who lived in Forest Park from the 1920s through the 1950s can leave Beth Tfiloh, Rabbi Rosenblatt, and Cantor Max Kotlowitz out of his or her memories. Marilyn Leavitt Colson's family moved to 3011 Garrison Boulevard, close to the synagogue (at 3200 Garrison at Fairview Avenue), in 1936. The Leavitts had been living on Liberty Heights Avenue near Burleith Avenue and were already members of Beth Tfiloh. And that is probably why, Leavitt family consensus holds, the family bought the house in Forest Park some years earlier and then moved to it in 1936. Meanwhile, Tifereth Israel Synagogue, at Garrison Avenue and Forest Park Avenue, commanded its own loyal, if smaller, following.

The movie theater that became the "neighborhood movie" in Forest Park was the Forest. The Forest opened in 1922, seating 650 and charging twenty cents for matinees, forty cents for evening performances. Its architecture still lingers in memories: Italian Romanesque, red brick roof with green tile, a small foyer of red brick trimmed with white marble and a marble floor. The last show was *On the Waterfront* with Marlon Brando on Saturday, May 13, 1961.

The Ambassador opened in 1935 at 4604 Liberty Heights Avenue with *Page Miss Glory*, starring Marion Davies, Dick Powell, and Pat O'Brien. It was thought to be the first really modern and thoroughly art deco movie house built in Baltimore. The last movie shown there was *The Fox*, on October 8, 1968.

With its cluster of public schools, Forest Park was like a self-contained village, providing families with kindergarten through elementary and junior high through high school, all within a square-mile area. Dyed-in-the-wool Forest Parkers attended P.S. 64 elementary school at Maine and Garrison Avenues, then Garrison Junior High at Garrison Boulevard and Barrington Road, then Forest Park High at Eldorado Avenue and Chatham Road. Pearl Neiman Shiling followed this path. She says, "I never, ever, through all of my years of public schooling—elementary, junior high, senior high—took a streetcar or bus to school. I walked every day!"

Birdie Falk Hack was another Forest Park graduate who attended the neighborhood schools. When she was five months old, her family moved from South Baltimore to 4004 Springdale Avenue in 1925, where she says

Right: The very first graduating class of the Isaac Davidson Hebrew School in 1930. *First row, left to right:* Rena Sharp Sugar, Herbert Klein, Elsie Shpritz Berger. *Top row:* Emanuel Katz, Ada Sauber Winakur, Leonard Woolf.

Right, facing page: Hymen Saye, teaching a class at the Baltimore Talmud Torah at 1029 East Baltimore Street, in 1928. By the 1930s there were six Talmud Torahs serving the Baltimore Jewish community: Baltimore Talmud Torah, at 22 North Broadway; Northwest, at Callow Avenue and Lennox Street; Southwest, at Eagle and Payson Street; Western, at 743 West Lexington Street; South Baltimore, at 518 South Hanover Street; and Isaac Davidson, at Shirley Avenue between Park Heights Avenue and Reisterstown Road. Alumnus Melvin Sykes says of the Talmud Torahs: "There is just no comparison with the curriculum of religious schools today with that of the Talmud Torahs. Their curriculum was two hours a day, five days a week, and included study of the Five Books of Moses, Siddur, Joshua, Judges, Kings, laws, history, literature, and Hebrew."

Isaac Davidson Hebrew School Consecra-
tion Class, 1960. Two years later, the building was vacated and the students were
transferred to Petach Tikvah synagogue.
The school itself closed officially in 1967.

Max Hoffman's tailor shop at 1700 McKean Avenue, 1937. Many immigrant Jews had been engaged in tailoring in Eastern Europe, and those who could brought their sewing machines to America with them. So equipped, they were desirable employees to German Jewish clothing manufacturers—some of whom even met them at Locust Point. The manufacturers were quick to offer jobs, and immigrants were quick to take them. But the time came when many in this group, wearied of the working conditions, opened their own shops. Between the World Wars, most every Jewish neighborhood had a "tailor shop."

Summer camps were popular among Balti-
more Jewish families. There were many
nearby, but some families were able to send
their children off to upstate New York and
New England. Camp Wigwam for Boys, in
Harrison, Maine (through which flowed
"Mutiny Brook"), drew many campers from
Baltimore's German Jewish community.

Facing page: Snapshots (and memories) of
Camp Tripp Lake in Maine, c. 1919. Among
members of the field hockey squad, Marie
Lowenstein stands on the left. As part of a
camp pageant, the girls re-enacted an at-
tack on a pioneer settlement.

GIANTS HOCKEY.

Intent listeners wait for a moment with a
"fortune teller" at a YM and YWHA summer
camp in 1952. Early on, the Associated Jewish Charities provided educational and
recreational opportunities for Jewish
youth. Through the years it supported Camp
Airy and Camp Louise, the Jewish Community Centers, and any number of efforts that
encouraged Jewish education and recreation programs for the young.

The girls of Camp Louise, Frederick County, Maryland, 1927. In 1922, Aaron and Lillie Straus acquired a camp in the Catoctin Mountains not far from Thurmont and re- named it Camp Louise—for Mr. Straus's sister, Louise. In 1924, they established nearby Camp Airy as a site for boys. Their largess made it possible for generations of young Jewish children whose parents could not afford the full costs of summer camp to trade the summer heat of the city for the cool glades of Western Maryland.

her parents rented out the upstairs. "I remember more about school P.S. 64 than I do about college, Goucher, and I remained friendly all my life with people I met in my kindergarten class. I remember Myra Askin, who lived at 3306 Springdale, Betty Ford Mazer, Howard Offit, Sylvan Offit, Leroy Hoffberger, William Kahn, Marcia Gann Pines, Shirley Cohen Lessans, Lee Vogelstein. From kindergarten through sixth grade, my teachers were, successively, Miss Smith, Miss Ada, Miss Lewis, Mrs. Carpenter, Mrs. Williams, Mrs. Davies, and Mrs. Kirkely."

Others who went the route of P.S. 64, Garrison, then Forest Park included Sylvan Offit and Elaine Cohen Weinstein. In 1929 the Davises—Paul, Marvin (now Dr. Marvin Davis) and Bette (now Bette Davis Cohen) moved to 3705 Garrison Boulevard and rented the upstairs apartment to help pay the mortgage. Marvin recalls neighbors David Tissenbaum, Joshua Breshkin, Myron Myers, Marvin Freeman, Mose Ottenheimer, Eugene Feinblatt, and I. H. "Bud" Hammerman. "Best of all," Dr. Davis says, "I always looked forward to walking to school with the very beautiful Margaret Hayes, who quite predictably went on to Hollywood stardom." Dr. Davis is talking about a girl he knew as Florette Ottenheimer, who attended P.S. 64 and Forest Park High, graduating as a teacher from Johns Hopkins University. She became the first woman to act in the Hopkins Barnstormers, where women's roles had been, up until then, taken by male students dressed as women. Winning fame under the name Margaret Hayes, she is best remembered for her role in the movie *Blackboard Jungle*.

Sylvan Offit's family moved from Caroline Street to 3223 Vickers Road in Forest Park in 1923. The house was a duplex; the family lived on the first floor and rented out the second. He too went to P.S. 64 and Garrison Junior High, graduating from Forest Park High in 1943. Like most of the neighborhood young people, he spent a lot of time at Beth Tfiloh at club meetings, on the basketball court, and at dances.

"Birdie Falk was my first date," Sylvan recalls. "We were all members of 'The Blue Stars,' and mostly we played basketball. There were about twenty-five of us—Howard Offit, Morty Offit, Alan Schapiro, Roy Brenner, Teddy Schwartzman, Albert Perlow. Michael Kitt was the director of the activities, Howard Shpritz was our Hebrew teacher. We loved to walk to the Ambassador; it was beautiful, high class. The Forest and the Gwynn were like broken-down barns compared to the Ambassador."

The Reuben Levensons moved from Lakeview Avenue to 3306 Springdale Avenue in 1928. Myra Levenson Askin says, "I remember that in each of the four houses directly across the street from us was a Hoffberger—Saul,

Jack, Abe, and Charles. I was in the 'Just Pals' club at Beth Tfiloh with Birdie Falk Hack, Elaine Cohen Weinstein, and Phyllis Cooper Schaeffer. Although my father was Russian, my mother was German, so we split our time between Beth Tfiloh and Baltimore Hebrew."

Another center for young people was Branch 14 of the Enoch Pratt Library at Garrison Boulevard and Fairview, catty-corner to Beth Tfiloh. Marilyn Leavitt Colson recalls going there often. "We walked there most every day after school." Mrs. Hack says, "It was the most quiet, most peaceful place on earth. A whisper in there would bring a cold, withering stare from the librarian." Pearl Neiman Shiling moved to 4114 Fairview Avenue near Beth Tfiloh and the library in the early 1920s, from Fairmount Avenue in East Baltimore. "I lived in that library. It was heaven," she says. "In the summers, before I was old enough to go to camp, I spent most of the day there."

The neighborhood bowling alley, too, was popular. Howard Berman moved to 3015 Garrison Boulevard (near Beth Tfiloh) in 1939. He remembers Friday nights in the Forest Park of his teens. "We often congregated at the bowling alley. It was on Garrison Boulevard at about Forest Park Avenue. A group of us, probably including at one time or another Doug Dixon, Henry Honick, Jerry Scher, Don Dagold, Mark Rosenfield, and Herb Seidman. By the way, those were the days before pins were set automatically and 'pinboys' did the setting up of the pins. After we had bowled a few games we would walk over to Paul's deli. That's where we'd see even more of the gang from the neighborhood. Paul's during the early 1940s was our Nates and Leon's 'uptown.'"

Forest Park, like many Jewish neighborhoods, had its own shopping centers. Visiting them often, patrons had made them into neighborhood institutions. There were two concentrations of stores; one at Liberty Heights and Garrison wrapping around Ayrdale Avenue; the other, Garrison Boulevard at Belle Avenue. On a bright Sunday afternoon in January 1998, sixty years after they had last shopped in those stores, Bette Davis Cohen and her brother, Dr. Marvin Davis, visited the shopping center that was no more.

"Right there," Mrs. Cohen says as she points to 3831 Garrison Boulevard, "was Kelly's Drug Store. On the second floor was Dr. Leon Seligman, the dentist. And there, two doors down, was Surosky's, the kosher butcher." Sylvan Surosky confirms the recollection. He and his brother David had operated the shop from 1934 through 1970. "Though most of our trade was walk-in traffic from the neighborhood, as people moved out of

Forest Park, they continued to phone in their orders to us," he says. "We'd deliver anywhere the same day. And there was plenty of competition for the business. Barr's was over at Liberty Heights Avenue, and Posner's was over on Ayrdale."

Further along, Mrs. Cohen points to a house and remembers: "Something about that house—oh, yes. On the lawn of that house was a sign, 'No Jews or Dogs Allowed.' That was in 1935."

Approaching the intersection where Garrison Boulevard meets Liberty Heights Avenue, Dr. Davis quickly creates a snapshot of all four corners, circa 1940. "On the left, Read's. On the right, the church is still there. Over there, the northwest corner, is the firehouse, and close to it, the Forest movie—the shell of it is still there. On the southwest corner, Lambros Liquors." Beyond the Forest was Wagner's Pharmacy. "On that corner every spring a Filipino put on a yo-yo demonstration." Across Garrison were, among other stores, Silber's, Gottlieb's, and Loft's Candy." Mrs. Cohen recalls, "And starting down at Ayrdale, Shure's Drugs, Kresge's Five and Ten, Nathan Stein's Billiard Parlor, C & L Delicatessen, Duane Bakery, the A&P, Martha Washington Candies, Arundel Ice Cream. All long gone." Missing, too, from the street are not just the stores that were part of the lifestyle of the neighborhood, Dr. Davis notes, but "the streetcars rumbling along Liberty Heights and Garrison Boulevard."

Forest Park as a Jewish community lasted less than forty years. In those brief, bright, fleeting years, thousands of men and women, who are today in their fifties and older, went through their rites of passage on Forest Park's tree-lined streets, in Branch 14 library, in the neighborhood's schools, stores and movies, in the binding mystique of shared experiences, and in the nurturing comfort of Beth Tfiloh's warm embrace.

Jack Pollack: Master of the Game

In a century of Baltimore Jewish history no more controversial figure exists than James H. "Jack" Pollack. More than twenty years after his death, the effect of the power he wielded is still debated. What are we to make of this up-from-the streets East Baltimore ex-boxer and obsessive political warrior who was also a husband, father, and family man? From the 1920s through at least the late 1960s, Jack Pollack held absolute control over the Fourth District's twenty-five thousand plus voting Jewish Democrats, and he leveraged that bloc of power to gain influence at the very highest levels of City Hall, the State House, and the courthouse.

To understand Jack Pollack, one needs to appreciate the sheer size of his presence fifty years ago. In one way or another, he touched the lives of most Jews who were living in Baltimore from the 1930s through the 1960s. That's because life in the poor and middle classes—and, in many cases, even the upper class—of Northwest Baltimore was linked to the patronage system. There was a fair exchange in the marketplace: in return for your vote, Mr. Pollack got you (or your son or relative) a job or whatever else you might need that government could give you. Largess to loyalists was the game; in Northwest Baltimore Jack Pollack was master of that game.

Jack Pollack was born on October 21, 1899, in a two-story brick house on Watson Street in East Baltimore, the fifth child of Russian-Jewish immigrants Moses and Rachel Pollackoff. The family attended synagogue regularly and kept kosher. But when Jack was sixteen, his mother died and his father remarried; from that point on, the household seems to have been a troubled one.

Mr. Pollack learned early the street smarts he would need to outflank the establishment on his way to wealth and power. A young Jack Pollack rejected the mainstream's focus on education. Bored with school and weary of working at a stitching machine in his father's East Baltimore clothing workshop, he dropped out of school in the fifth grade. He ran away, moved in with his sister, sold newspapers, and very quickly became integrated into the street life of East Baltimore, brushing up against the Irish and Polish gangs. Fighting was a way of life, and he attempted to improve his lot by taking boxing lessons at the Jewish Educational Alliance. He became a professional and toured the country, even boxing in a preliminary to a Jack Dempsey fight.

After two years he returned to Baltimore with little to show for his efforts except bruised and swollen hands, which he would display and talk about the rest of his life. Pollack's streetwise sensibilities and Prohibition combined to provide a money-making opportunity. With the law looking the other way, Pollack and some of his peers did business profitably and comfortably as bootleggers. When Prohibition ended in 1933, Mr. Pollack was thought to be a wealthy man. In an attempt to become part of the "establishment," he opened the James H. Pollack Insurance Agency. Insurance was to serve as Mr. Pollack's official business for the next forty some years.

Meanwhile, the late 1920s, when Mr. Pollack entered the world of local politics, was a time of turmoil and change in Baltimore and Maryland. By 1920, John J. "Sonny" Mahon and Frank S. Kelly controlled all of the votes in the Baltimore City Council. Mayor Howard Jackson, with the backing of Governor Albert C. Ritchie, put together a rival organization aimed at eliminating the influence of Mr. Mahon and Mr. Kelly. But fate intervened: Mr. Mahon and Mr. Kelly both died in the same year, 1928. Kelly's lieutenant, William "Machiavelli" Curran, stepped up and assumed command. By his side he found an energetic and savvy loyalist, Jack Pollack. A large part of the city's patronage now would be handed out by an Irish Catholic from the East Side's Third District and a Jew from Northwest Baltimore's Fourth District.

Mr. Pollack rose quickly in the new organization, and as soon as he felt he could, he left Mr. Curran. By the mid-1930s Mr. Pollack had taken over the moribund Trenton Democratic Club at 3701 Park Heights Avenue. The day he opened that door he opened a whole new era for Baltimore and the Baltimore Jewish community. Among those who won elections with Pollack's support were Murray Abramson, Jerome Robinson, Leon Rubinstein, Maurice Cardin, Jacob Edelman, Sam Friedel, Bernard Melnicove, Solomon Liss, Reuben Caplan, Richard Rombro, Sol Friedman, and Albert Sklar.

In 1959 Mr. Pollack was at the height of his glory, in a role that State Delegate Paul Weisengoff would later describe as "the most successful political leader the city is going to know." But where Mr. Weisengoff saw success, the *Sun* saw a looming civic crisis. The occasion was the mayoral primary that saw Thomas D'Alesandro, Jr., running against J. Harold Grady. The *Sun* viewed the election as the electorate's opportunity to give Mr. Pollack a sound shellacking, his comeuppance, and to "loosen the Pollack grip" once and for all, by rejecting Mr. Pollack's hand-picked candidate, Thomas D'Alesandro, Jr. And Mr. D'Alesandro did, in fact, lose the election to the "Three Gs"—J. Harold Grady, R. Walter Graham, and Philip Goodman. History will show that this lost election in 1959 was one of several factors that together brought Jack Pollack's legendary career into its waning days.

The first and largest of the factors was the changing racial makeup of the Fourth District, which was losing its predominantly Jewish base. In 1954, five years before the epochal election in which the *Sun* went to the mat with Mr. Pollack, election results foreshadowed the demise of the all-white political alliances in Baltimore City. Republican Harry Cole became the first African American elected to the State Senate, Emory Cole defeated a Pollack candidate for the House of Delegates, and Truly Hatchet, an African American from Pollack's Fourth District, won another seat in the House of Delegates.

Stung, Pollack moved his base to the Fifth District, where much of his constituency had moved. In 1957, acting defensively, he formed the Town and Country Democratic Club. But he was never to have the consummate power in the Fifth which he had known in the Fourth. By 1958, African Americans had taken control of the elected offices in the Fourth. Many Jewish politicians, sensing the end, deserted Pollack. Among the earliest to leave the master were Delegate Murray Abramson and Councilman Alex Stark. In 1962 four members of the State Legislature, including Marvin Mandel, chairman of the city delegation, cut the cord. Political observers were quick to call Pollack "washed up"—probably prematurely, although it's uncertain what power Pollack still held in his last days.

Pollack died on March 14, 1977, at University Hospital after a long bout with cancer. He was seventy-seven. Congressman Benjamin Cardin said of Mr. Pollack at the time of his death, "He was a man who laid the groundwork for political power by looking after his people during the Depression."

In addressing the controversy surrounding his reputation, Mr. Pollack once said of himself, "The allegations of my legendary leadership are greatly exaggerated. However, it is an honor no gentleman should decline." These words do not appear on Mr. Pollack's tombstone, but perhaps they should. It's been forty-five years since Harry Cole became the first African American to upset the Pollack machine in the Fourth District, forty years after the *Sun* took on Mr. Pollack with all the power of its editorials, and more than twenty years since Mr. Pollack died. That would seem to be enough distance to examine the Pollack legacy and fix its place in the history of the Baltimore Jewish community.

MANY, INCLUDING THOSE who thought themselves close to him, do not remember Pollack fondly. But this group of wary skeptics say that, out of respect for the family and after only twenty years have gone by, they want to remain anonymous. All make the same allusions to his vindictiveness and to the accusations of corruption: that he made his influence felt in zoning cases; that he sought favors through the judiciary; that he got wealthy through use of his political power.

Bradford Jacobs, late editor of the *Evening Sun*, followed Mr. Pollack's career almost from beginning to end. He said, "Jack Pollack produced the best delegations in Annapolis and at City Hall. Pollack men always seemed smarter than their counterparts from other districts, and in that sense, he rendered a genuine service to the city." Reuben Shiling, a well-known attorney and observer of the scene, confirmed Mr. Jacobs' recollection. "The Pollack delegation was committed to Pollack on purely political issues. But in fairness to him, he did not interfere on non-political issues. In fact, the delegation, in keeping with the Jewish tradition, could be counted on to take the lead in the enactment of progressive legislation, in the areas of education, health, welfare of the poor."

Mr. Jacobs recalled that for all that, Pollack kept his delegates "terrified." "He'd let them go any way they wanted until it came to patronage," he said, adding:

> I watched election returns come in from all over the city. Results would go this way and that, and then the Fourth District would come in—and wham! They'd hit for Pollack candidates solid, like a ton of concrete! Three hundred to six! Four hundred and fifty to ten! When the Fourth came in, elections turned around!
>
> In some ways, I have to put Pollack down on the bad side, but in other ways, well, he brought Jewish smarts into focus for many good purposes.

Jerry Kelly, a former reporter for the *Evening Sun*, says, "He is a chapter in our local political history. He was a major influence and profited as much as anyone he deigned to help. He was a successful insurance man. He didn't need a ticket to get in wherever power was respected."

On the afternoon of May 16, 1985, an auctioneer stood on the porch of a semi-detached house on the northeast corner of Park Heights and Violet Avenues and sought to tease up the price. "Gentlemen, gentlemen," he intoned. "Please, there're millions of dollars of memories here." The Trenton Democratic Club's famous headquarters was on the auction block. The auctioneer had overestimated the crowd's evaluation of those memories: when the bidding got to $10,000 it froze.

The auctioneer's voice grew more pleading. Talking about Mr. Pollack's son, he said, "Morton Pollack has decided to absolutely change ownership today. Come gentlemen, Jack would never let this house of history go for only ten thousand dollars. That would not be the way he wanted it. Do I hear eleven thousand dollars?"

"I was here as a boy all the time," a hanger-on observed. "You talk about crowds, it was wall-to-wall. Pollack was king." At long last, the auctioneer, scanning the crowd for a signal from someone to up the bid, gave in. "Sold!" he said, "to the gentleman for eleven thousand dollars." The gentleman was James Rockett, a real estate investor. The hanger-on murmured, "Good thing Pollack is dead. He'd be madder than hell."

The crowd understood. Jack Pollack finally had lost control.

The Talmud Torahs: "A Shining Page in Local Jewish History"

Jewish education the way it was.

Today there are approximately 12,000 children enrolled in the synagogue-affiliated religious schools of Baltimore's Center for Jewish Education system, successor to the Baltimore Board of Jewish Education. They attend classes in sixty-five separate schools that offer diverse curricula and Jewish lifestyles, ranging from Modern Orthodox through Conservative, Reform, and Reconstructionist.

This burgeoning system is the successor to the old Talmud Torahs, which never listed more than six separate schools and served no more than fifteen hundred students at any given time. But the Talmud Torahs made up Baltimore's first highly visible, community-wide system committed to providing a Jewish education for Baltimore's Jewish children. Before the Talmud Torahs, Jewish education had been left mainly to private tutors of varying abilities, education levels, personalities, and characters, with notions of discipline that relied heavily on punishment—mental and physical. According to Harry London, a student and educator in that Jewish education system, "There was clearly a need for more order, system, and structure, and for more professionalism in teacher methods, curriculum planning, supervision, and teacher training. In addition, there was a need for schools where girls could be comfortably included. Enter the Talmud Torahs."

The first Talmud Torah opened in 1889. There were six in the system when they closed in the years following World War II. In between, they created a record of accomplishment and set a standard of excellence for Jewish education that yesterday's graduates and today's educators look back on with fondness and awe. Melvin Sykes attended the Baltimore Talmud Torah at 22 North Broadway from 1930 to 1936. He says:

There is just no comparison with the curriculum of religious schools today and that of the Talmud Torahs. Their curriculum was two hours a day, five days a week, and included study of the Five Books of Moses, Siddur, Joshua, Judges, Kings, laws, history, literature, and Hebrew.

Today the children who do not attend day schools may go two or at the most three days a week. They can't possibly learn in two or three days what we learned in five. I was always unhappy that the Talmud Torahs closed, but their closing was inevitable, for at least two reasons. First, the community fragmented along denominational lines, and synagogue schools replaced the community Talmud Torahs. The synagogues wanted to control the education of their members' children. Second, parents' priorities today are different, their lifestyle is different. In those days you could walk to school, or travel by street-car. Today the parents have to commit to a lot of chauffeuring and have to choose between Hebrew school, ballet, and Little League. Little League wins a lot.

In my class were Joe, now Judge, Pines, who was the catcher on the school's softball team, and Isaac Rehert, longtime feature writer with the *Sun*. Some of the teachers I remember included Sriah Shoubin, Shoshana Cardin's father, and Abe Lesser and Benjamin Udoff, Miss Deborah Schochet, Miss Leah Greenberg. Principals included Morris Seidel—that was Herman's brother—and Perez Tarshish.

According to Hymen Saye, who is an alumnus of the Baltimore Talmud Torah and the Baltimore Hebrew College, the Baltimore Talmud Torah in the early days of this century was one of the most famous Hebrew schools of the American Jewish community. Dr. Raymond Bloom, writing in his doctoral dissertation, observed, "It rivaled the famous Uptown Talmud Torah of New York." The school was founded in 1889 in a "rented room"; 21 North High Street is given as its first address, 1017 East Baltimore Street as its second. The six Talmud Torahs serving the Baltimore Jewish community were: Baltimore Talmud Torah, 22 North Broadway; Northwest, Callow Avenue and Lennox Street; Southwest, at Eagle and Payson Streets; Western, at 743 West Lexington Street; South Baltimore, at 518 South Hanover Street; and Isaac Davidson, on Shirley Avenue between Park Heights Avenue and Reisterstown Road. Harold "Hal" Schlaffer attended the Northwest Talmud Torah from 1940 through 1945, "from the first grade to the last grade." He recalls:

I went Monday through Thursday, and Sunday mornings, straight through the summer. There was maybe a brief vacation in there somewhere.

We didn't color, we didn't do arts and crafts. We sat and we studied. Yiddish, *davening*, *chumash*. We didn't spend a minute on "customs" because you were expected to learn that at home.

Lapses of memory, inattention, and failure to do homework often brought a smack on the fingers with a ruler. The fun time was slim but quite memorable. We would all go out to Gwynn Oak Park for a picnic, and play in the very competitive softball league. I played with Mannie

Sklar, Victor Marder, Bill Saltzman, Arnold Weiner. We had an annual Chanukah party at the Lyric complete with magicians and songs and plays. At the end of the show, as you left, a teacher would hand you a Chanukah gift.

I still carry the memory of leaving the Lyric and of a teacher handing me a gift. The teacher was my father.

Dr. Barnett Berman was a student at the Southwest Talmud Torah at Payson and Eagle Streets in the 1930s. He looks back:

About those softball games, I vividly remember the spirit and rivalry of the inter-school softball league. Our home field was Carroll Park. Away games were played in Patterson Park with Baltimore Talmud Torah, and on the P.S. 59 lot across from Isaac Davidson.

It appears to me that Western Talmud Torah and Baltimore Talmud Torah were seldom forces within the league. Year after year the championship was bitterly contested by Simon Bugatch's Southwestern Talmud Torah and the feared Sidney Esterson's Isaac Davidson.

As alumni are fond of reminding themselves, Talmud Torah classes were held five days weekly. Each pupil attended four days a week in two-hour shifts, either from 4:00 to 6:00 P.M. or from 6:00 to 8:00 P.M. Hymen Saye remembered, "During all my Hebrew school years, I never had dinner with my family because I was always in the 6:00 to 8:00 P.M. shift." Classes were held on Sundays from 9:00 to 11:00 A.M. and from 11:00 A.M. to 1:00 P.M. There appeared to be plenty to do after class on Sundays—a Hebrew speaking club, Young Judea Club, dramatics.

Harry London, who attended Isaac Davidson from 1929 to 1934, remembers that the best students of the Baltimore Hebrew College came from the graduates of the Talmud Torahs, and the first of the locally born, locally trained teachers who staffed the classrooms of Baltimore's Hebrew schools drew from their ranks. Mr. Saye had said, "Some of them went on to become the principals and educational directors collaborating with Dr. Louis Kaplan in creating a system of schools which is still nourishing the Jewish spirit of our community."

After World War II, for a variety of reasons, the synagogues wanted to keep their own members and their members' children closer to their respective institutions, and so they opened their own schools. The era of the five-day-a-week after school Hebrew education in a partnership with the secular public school system had come to an end. But the system remains a historically important model for, among other things, parental commitment to Jewish education.

Of the era of the Talmud Torahs, Hymen Saye concluded, "It was a shining page in local Jewish history."

The *Exodus*: Sailing Out of Baltimore and into History

Ordinary people with extraordinary passion lived out this historic saga.

On a cold (twenty-one degrees), windy, and moonless night in February 1947, a Pennsylvania Railroad freight train ground to a standstill at the President Street Station on Aliceanna Street, east of the Inner Harbor and a block north of Baltimore's Lancaster Street waterfront. Out of the shadows, a truck maneuvered to even itself with a boxcar's doors, then cut its lights. Within seconds, workmen jumped off the truck and began unloading the boxcar. They formed a human chain, passing the cartons to one another until the boxcar was empty and the truck full.

The truck, with men and cargo aboard, was driven a block due south to Pier 8, Lancaster Street, and came to a stop at the gangway of a ship moored along the quay. There, in the dark, the same workmen unloaded what only a few minutes before they had loaded, forming the same man-to-man chain and stowing the cartons aboard. Curiously, the ship, with the name *President Warfield* on its bow, flew the flag of Honduras.

John Pica, now in his seventies and living in Baltimore, was one of those workmen. "We loaded the ship every night for weeks. We were Italian boys from Little Italy and Jewish guys from the JEA, the Jewish Educational Alliance over on Central Avenue," he said. "We grew up together and after the war we hung out together. The Jewish guys asked us to help them unload trains and take the stuff aboard a ship. Charlie Rosen, who had a bar on Lancaster Street, asked me to help. He told me that the ship was going to Palestine. But we didn't care about that. Our Jewish buddies had asked us to help load that ship, and we did."

In recollection half a century later, that scene takes on the look of a Hollywood movie in the making, with the Baltimore waterfront as a setting. But in fact, the secretive unloading of trains and loading of trucks, the run over to the Lancaster Street dock to load the ship, was real-life drama. In violation of who knows how many laws, men had been recruited to fit out a ship for a clandestine voyage. The cargo was a mix of guns, ammunition, diapers, medicines, dehydrated food—all obtained illegally, received from nonexistent sources, bound for nonexistent addresses. The ship, through a complex series of faked papers, had been declared as a vessel going to China, but she was really on her way to Palestine. Within months, Jews the world over would know that the S.S. *President Warfield* was going to start her legendary journey out of Baltimore, bound for Palestine and a place in history. She would be known in song and story as the *Exodus*.

Her beginnings were inauspicious. When she left Baltimore on February 24, 1947, from Pier 5, she immediately ran into bad weather and had to be towed. She limped into Hampton Roads, Virginia. She finally made it to Sète, France, where she took on refugees, and then set sail for Palestine. As she neared Tel Aviv, British destroyers pulled up alongside, flooded the ship with light, and ordered it to Haifa. In defiance, the refugees held up a huge plank displaying the name *President Warfield,* and then promptly flipped it over to show the reverse side, *Haganah Ship Exodus, 1947.* The blue and white Zionist flag, now the flag of Israel, could be seen raised to the top of the mast.

The British forced the ship to Haifa. Her passengers were ordered off for immediate reboarding onto British ships for return to France, which had opened its doors to Jewish refugees. When the Jewish passengers of the *Exodus* refused to disembark, blatantly disobeying the British orders, the ship was ordered to Germany.

THE STORY of the *Exodus* is a Baltimore story. In the center of it was Baltimore Jewish businessman Mose Speert. On the occasion of the twentieth anniversary of the *Exodus'* (S.S. *President Warfield's*) departure from Baltimore, Mr. Speert reminisced with friends and reporters. "It all started one sweltering day in New York in 1945 in the apartment of Rudolf Sonneborn, former Baltimorean and member of the Sonneborn family, which had once owned and operated the Baltimore-headquartered Sonneborn clothing manufacturing company."

Mr. Speert explained how Mr. Sonneborn had called together about fifteen American businessmen and Zionist leaders concerned about the fate of European Jewry to hear a report on the situation by David Ben Gurion:

> Ben Gurion pulled no punches. He told us money and supplies were vital to save those European Jews who could still be saved. We were sworn to secrecy. There were two of us from Baltimore, Adolph Hamburger and myself. We pledged to help.
>
> Since we were breaching the British mandatory powers we had to

work undercover, raise the money privately, make our own contacts. We never told anyone what the money and supplies were for. Never gave any receipts, never kept accounts.

People all over the country contributed. Zionists, non-Zionists, Jews and non-Jews. And it was all done secretly—there were no tax deductions. And no one outside the small circle, even in a small, closely-knit community like Baltimore, had any idea what we were up to.

As long as we worked quietly, if we didn't flaunt what we were doing, we were left alone. I was storing stuff in my warehouse on Hanover Street, but I know my phone was tapped. And there was always a tail on me.

The refitting was done over months while the ship was tied up at Pier 5, known as Long Dock, just offshore from the Power Plant and west of Pier 6, familiar today as the site of a concert pavilion. H. Graham Wood, a national authority on Chesapeake Bay steamboats, had visited the ship at Long Dock before its journey. He said, "I surmised that the owners had other plans when I noticed a supply of life preservers and mess kits aboard and the appearance of the crew. Save for the captain, there was ample evidence that they were mostly all Jewish."

The S.S. *President Warfield* had been making overnight excursions down the Chesapeake Bay to Norfolk, Virginia, for more than a decade prior to her adventure as the *Exodus*. Baltimoreans will recall that she departed from Baltimore Harbor on alternate afternoons at 5:30. Aboard for these trips were vacationers and business types, all enjoying comfortable dining and accommodations. Then in 1942 the *Warfield* was pressed into wartime service. She was stripped of the chintz, glittering chandeliers, shining mirrors, mahogany trim, and all her finery and converted for service as an Allied troopship. The S.S. *President Warfield* became the U.S.S. *President Warfield*.

In 1945, the war-weary, worn-out hulk was sold for scrap. In October of 1946 she was bought for $40,000 by a mysterious organization calling itself "Western Trading Corporation" and then (just as mysteriously) transferred to Panamanian registry. "She virtually had to be rebuilt," Mr. Speert recalled. "We painted her gray for the simple reason that the only color paint we had was gray.

"We set up an infirmary, an operating room, even a delivery room. With forty-five hundred people aboard in spaces built to accommodate two hundred and fifty, we knew we were bound to have some pregnant women before this thing was over." Dr. Herman Seidel was, at the time, among Baltimore's and the country's most active Zionists. "My job," he said in a 1967 interview, "was to give medical checkups to the volunteers who came to Baltimore from all over this country and Canada. A number of Baltimoreans helped me. They included Herman Speert, Reuben Levenson, Ben Katzner, Elkan Myers, Joseph Allen, Samuel J. Keiser, Henry Kuntz, Samuel Shapiro—to name some but surely not all."

Mr. Speert recalled how his small group of dedicated Zionists and non-Zionists, Jews and non-Jews, got hold of buckets for use as temporary toilet facilities; built bunks out of twelve-inch boards and arranged them in layers four or five deep; collected nails, rope, lumber, diapers, medicines, and foodstuffs such as dehydrated apples, milk, eggs, baby food, even kosher food:

We tried to make sure the passengers had a cooked meal every three days. The water for drinking and washing was bought in two-quart cans. Each can was worth its weight in gold.

Some of the supplies were donated. Much of it was army surplus. It seemed to be understood that the army and the FBI were well aware of what was going on. And until the supplies could be safely stored aboard, all of it—including guns and ammunition—was secretly stored in the warehouse of my business, Maryland Distillery Products, on Hanover Street at Lombard.

Acquiring supplies was difficult. This was supposed to be a ship carrying freight and things like diapers and baby food were not usually found as freight. And so getting supplies on board was a challenge, because it all had to be done under government inspection.

But, Mr. Speert insisted, "We managed to talk our way through one way or another. We set up dummy companies which we contrived to cable us for this and that extraordinary item."

Edward Sandler, who had long been active in Baltimore Jewish affairs, remembered that in the winter of 1946 he visited the ship with his uncle, Robert Seff. "Mose Speert met us at the dock, where the ship was tied up, and ushered us aboard," Mr. Sandler recalled. "Once we were aboard he showed us how the ship was being converted from the troop ship she had been, berthing several hundred, to a ship designed to carry forty-five hundred. They were tearing down the staterooms and the bunk beds and building tiers of double bunks. When our tour was over Mr. Speert asked Mr. Seff for a contribution, which he gave on the spot, five hundred dollars in 1946 dollars."

Getting cargo was one thing, getting a crew together was another. Mr. Speert said that men came from all over the country to Baltimore. "Seamen, clerks, students. Lord knows how they all knew about the *Warfield* and its mission but they did, and they came."

Sailing date was set for Monday, February 24, 1947. A special send-off ceremony was held on Sunday, February 16. The *Sun* had bought into the deception and reported, "*Warfield*, Old Bay Line Queen, Exiled to China as a Riverboat." Each member of the crew was given a sweater, a Hebrew Bible, a Haganah flag, and a bottle of champagne, to be used when the ship would be renamed the *Exodus*. On Thursday afternoon, February 27, the *Evening Sun* reported that the S.S. *President Warfield* had departed from Pier 5, Canton. This time, however, reporters were getting the idea. The headline now read: "*President Warfield* Off on a Mystery Voyage."

Mystery voyage? Rumors were flying.

YEARS AFTER SHE PLAYED HER PART IN HISTORY, on August 26, 1952, the *Exodus* caught fire in Haifa harbor and was destroyed. All that remains of the legendary ship today are a few souvenirs, scattered about the world.

Everyone living in Baltimore—Jewish and non-Jewish alike—should drive over to Pratt Street by Pier 5, and then over to President Street, past the old station on Aliceanna Street, into Canton, to see where, half a century ago, ordinary people with extraordinary passion banded together to write the opening chapter in the historic saga of the *Exodus*, which sailed out of Baltimore and into history.

The Jews of Dundalk, Essex, Middle River: Living in Their Own Diaspora

Dundalk, Middle River, and Essex cannot be said to be your typical Jewish communities. These traditionally blue-collar neighborhoods of eastern Baltimore County are not known for kosher butchers, Hebrew book stores, Jewish community centers, or mikvehs. Relatively few Jews have reason to visit those neighborhoods; fewer still have ever lived there. But for approx-

B'nai Sholom was a Jewish island in a gentile sea.

imately fifty Jewish families who did live or work (or both) in these communities from the mid 1940s into the early 1960s, there was a synagogue—Reform Temple B'nai Sholom. From what one can gather from its records and from former members, it was a very active one, with vibrant programming that duplicated, in its fashion, the Jewish synagogue life more commonly experienced in Northwest Baltimore. Temple B'nai Sholom opened in 1948 and closed in 1982. In the years it operated, the temple offered its congregants a unique Jewish experience—life on a Jewish island in a gentile sea.

The synagogue came into being in 1948, when a group of Jewish families from Essex, Middle River, and Dundalk areas met at the Essex Community Center for their common cause: the need for Jews who find themselves living in a non-Jewish world to live and raise their children in the Jewish tradition. Frieda Sohn, an organizing member who then became principal and teacher in the religious school, expresses the need in human terms:

> One day my five-year-old daughter was playing with one of her many gentile friends when the friend said she could not play with my daughter the next morning, Sunday, because she had to go to church, and to the church's Sunday school. My daughter came home crying that she, too, wanted to go to a "church" school on Sunday. My husband, an aeronautical engineer, was working at Glenn L. Martin in Middle River, which is why we were living as Jews in the non-Jewish community of Middle River. But when my daughter began to confront the issue I knew the time had come to do something about it.

The machinery of Jewish organization began to grind.

According to congregant Lillian Baker, who wrote a brief history of the synagogue, "When the group met, there was a discussion on the question of what our religious affiliation should be. We voted to function as a Reform congregation, even though several members had Orthodox and Conservative backgrounds." Dr. Mordecai I. Soloff of the Baltimore Jewish Board of Education served as the first rabbi. When he left Baltimore, Dr. Samuel Glasner, also of the Board, succeeded him and stayed with Temple B'nai Sholom until 1955. From that point on, the congregation was served by students from the Hebrew Union College in Cincinnati. Members of the congregation took turns providing weekend accommodations for the students who officiated at the Friday night services. There were no Saturday services.

In those days, members Franklin and Annette Blank lived in Gardenville. Mrs. Blank explains, "We joined B'nai Israel for the same reason that most of its members joined. There were no synagogues east of Falls Road and B'nai Sholom was formed to accommodate those Jews who lived 'east,' and who felt the need to provide their children with a Jewish education but who didn't choose to drive the distance to the synagogues and schools in Northwest Baltimore."

The congregation met originally at the Victory Villa Community Center in Middle River. Later the synagogue conducted Sunday school classes at the Essex Seventh Day Adventist Church and in rented second-floor quarters on the 400 block of Eastern Avenue. In June 1951, the synagogue purchased a brick home at 1108 East Homberg Avenue in Essex. Dedication services were held in 1954, with Governor Theodore R. McKeldin as guest speaker.

Reading the synagogue's bulletin, *Temple Topics*, of November 1950, gives an insight into the energy of B'nai Sholom synagogue life. The Rabbi's Message: "The number of members who have been contributing of their time, energy and means for the success of our November 5 project points to the determination of our community to support, strengthen, and expand the activities of our congregation." The bulletin goes on to list events:

> November 3: "Lecture by Mr. Paul Yaffe, 'Is There a parent in the House?'"
> November 10: "Discussion will be led by the rabbi on the activities of our school."
> November 17: "8 P.M. Children's Services."
> November 24: "Second Adult Educational Lecture."
> December 1: "Second Annual Sisterhood Service."

The announcements end with the inevitable Jewish "Thanks to": "Thanks to Estelle Beitch for obtaining the services of the Eastern Enterprise for photographing our Simchas Torah service." And "Thanks to Mollie Chmar for her fine chairmanship of our October sisterhood meeting. The meeting was held as a joint one with the Essex Middle River Hadassah."

Dr. Phillip and Molly Chmar had two children and were living in Middle River, where Dr. Chmar's dental practice was located. "I came to Middle River as a bride," Mrs. Chmar says,

> But I am a Baltimorean and I knew full well the dilemma we were facing as Jews and raising children while living in Middle River.

In those days, just after the war, distances were greater, and living where we were we found it difficult to go back and forth to the Park Heights synagogues. So we did the best we could to build our own Jewish world within the larger gentile world. The result was that we became over time a very close knit group. Besides helping to create and support the synagogue, I personally organized the drive for the Associated Jewish Charities.

We had children educated in our Sunday school all the way through to Bar and Bat Mitzvah. We did what we could to hold our small Jewish community together.

Sadly, the effort was not enough. In the 1960s membership began to dwindle. Some left to help form Temple Emanuel in the Liberty Road–Pikesville area. Earlier, in 1956, members living in Aberdeen and Havre de Grace had left to establish their own synagogue closer to home. In June 1968, the congregation decided to sell its building because it could no longer keep up the mortgage payments. The remaining members held holiday services first in the Essex Methodist Church and then later at the home of Pauline Baker. Victor Kandel led the high holiday services from 1965 until the congregation's final days in 1982.

In the memories of many, B'nai Sholom was more than a synagogue; it was a statement by a small group of Jews living in their own diaspora that, against the odds, they would indeed be Jewish.

The Walk to Shul: The High Holy Day Procession

"On the High Holy Day mornings a procession of congregants would walk by our house on its way to Shaarei Tfiloh."

On one of the High Holy Days in the mid-1950s, a visiting rabbi, Rafael Posner, addressing the Young Couples services at Beth Tfiloh synagogue, selected that occasion to exhort the congregants: "Live near a shul." Harry London, cantor emeritus of Beth Am Synagogue in Reservoir Hill, was there. "It was given to us," he recalls, "as if it were the eleventh commandment." Five years earlier, Rabbi Posner would not have needed to issue the commandment. It was already being followed. Most of the Jews in Baltimore then were already living near a shul; they had been for many years.

Nostalgia for those walk-to-shul neighborhoods drew a busload of the curious on June 15, 1998, to journey from the Park Heights Jewish Community Center back to places in times past. Included on the tour: Shaarei Zion, 3459 Park Heights Avenue; Agudas Achim Anshe Sphard, 4239 Park

Heights Avenue; and Har Zion, 2014 West North Avenue. The tour, under the auspices of the Jewish Museum of Maryland and the Jewish Community Center, was led by Bernard Fishman, then the museum's director.

To those who lived in Lower Park Heights in the shadow of Shaarei Zion synagogue, from the 1920s through the 1940s, the Park Heights they knew is unrecognizable today. The stores along the 3500 block, where the neighborhood once shopped, are gone. Those who grew up going in and out of these stores thought the shops would be there forever. But "forever" doesn't mean what it used to: Thomas the butcher, Brenner's dairy products, Hartman's bakery, Krastman's hardware, Joe Lozinsky's grocery and delicatessen—they are no more. (Tarlow Furs happily still survives, at a downtown location.) The wrecking ball has turned the familiar bricks into rubble, and the trash trucks have hauled away memories of youth.

The Shaarei Zion congregation looms large in the history of Baltimore's Jewish community. In the 1920s it was the first synagogue to establish itself in the Lower Park Heights corridor at Hillsdale, and its presence (and that of Shearith Israel at Glen Avenue in Upper Park Heights, at about the same time) opened the floodgates to what later would be called, with good reason, "Rue de la shul." Shaarei Zion would conduct its first services in the now-familiar building at Park Heights Avenue at Hilldale Avenue in 1926.

Shaarei Zion drew families from Park Heights, Violet, Cottage, Ulman, Rockrose, and Suffolk Avenues, and from Reisterstown Road down as far as Carlin's Park, north as far as Springhill Avenue. For forty years, Rabbi Israel Tabak ruled over the congregation as a firm but benign dictator. The cantor for many years was the gentle Samuel Greenberg. The synagogue sold its Lower Park Heights building in 1966 to the Good Shepherd Baptist Church.

Agudas Achim Anshe Sphard had the bad luck of being located across the street from a popular neighborhood movie theater, hence the identifying reference that seems to stick to it, "the shul across from the Avalon." Former members who lived nearby (the 4000 to 4500 blocks of Park Heights Avenue and the streets that led into it, including Quantico, Oswego, Towanda, Shirley, and Boarman Avenues) recall its earlier locations at 4230 and 4303 and its later venue at 4239.

The Reuben Kipnis family lived at 4015 Park Heights Avenue and were long and loyal members. Elaine Kipnis Abrams recalls, "My grandfather, Jacob Mizen, was president when Louis Friedlander was rabbi, and my brother was a Bar Mitzvah there." Dr. David Kipnis confirms his sister's recollection: "It was 1940." Herbert Shofer, who became a Bar Mitzvah there in 1937, recalls, "The place was always in a state of noisy confusion. People were always talking, and walking in and out. The *shammus* had a wooden mallet, carved into the shape of a fist. Every few minutes he would bang it on his reading table, and shout, 'Shah! Quiet! Shah!'"

Agudas Achim sold its building to the Cornerstone Church of Christ in 1969, and the next year it was merged into the Randallstown Synagogue Center in Baltimore County. Years later, former congregants still identify Agudas Achim by its storied location, "across from the Avalon."

The Jews who left East Baltimore in the 1920s for the neighborhoods around West North Avenue left the memory of two institutions as their legacy. The first, the Easterwood Park Boys, is very much alive; the second, Har Zion synagogue, is not. The synagogue closed the doors of its North Avenue edifice in 1952. But before that unhappy day, and from the day it opened at 2014 West North Avenue for the High Holy Days in 1922, it was the center of a vibrant Jewish community that took in neighborhoods within the larger area—Pulaski and Payson Streets, Ruxton and Clifton Avenues.

Har Zion merged in 1956 with Tifereth Israel of Forest Park and became Har Zion Tifereth Israel. The combined synagogues were joined by Petach Tikvah of Denmore Avenue and at that point became Pickwick Jewish Center.

Shaarei Tfiloh was the geographical and spiritual heart of the Auchentoroly Terrace and Mondawmin neighborhoods. Is it sacrilege to suggest that God was predisposed to be especially kind to the Shaarei Tfiloh synagogue when He chose to place it on the western edge of the green and lovely vistas of Druid Hill Park? Sylvia Mandy recalls, "We lived on Holmes Avenue, alongside the shul. I will never forget *Kol Nidre* nights. The streets were blocked off and the windows of the shul were thrown open. In the dusk of the coming evening of Yom Kippur young people would sit out on the porches and listen to the sounds of the *Kol Nidre*."

Herb Goldman became a Bar Mitzvah at Shaarei Tfiloh in 1955. He remembers:

Rabbi Nathan Drazin was rabbi, Jacob Wahrman the cantor. We lived at 3226 Tioga Parkway, but what we thought of as our neighborhood took in Layton, Whittier, Bryant Avenues, all the way north to Anoka, south to Fulton Avenue.

On the High Holy Day mornings a procession of congregants would walk by our house on its way to Shaarei Tfiloh. The crowd swelled as it moved through the streets to the synagogue's entrance. All you could see for blocks around were the families, the Hirsh Goldbergs, Sol Kleins, Ruby Caplans, coming from every direction, joining the walk to Shaarei Tfiloh.

CHANGE CAME TO THOSE NEIGHBORHOODS beginning in the early 1950s. The congregants moved further out, and most of the synagogues (excepting Shaarei Tfiloh) closed their doors forever or followed others out by building new edifices in the suburbs or by merging with another synagogue that had already left. Living near the shul is no longer the lifestyle of most in the Jewish community. Yet nostalgia for the way of life endures even among those who have abandoned it.

Bluefeld: King of the Kosher Caterers

For almost half a century, "Bluefeld" dominated the kosher catering business in Baltimore.

On the night of January 7, 1982, a very exclusive affair was taking place in the Carriage House at the Johns Hopkins University Evergreen House. Flowers were everywhere. White-gloved waiters hovered about; secret service agents with their ever-present earphones stood silently by. The host was Yitzhak Navon, the President of Israel. International dignitaries included Moshe Ahrens, Israel's Ambassador to the United States, and Samuel Lewis, United States Ambassador to Israel. In attendance in behalf of the Johns Hopkins University was University President Steven Muller. Representing local Jewish organizations were Joseph Meyerhoff, Harvey "Bud" Meyerhoff, and Jerry Hoffberger. Governor Harry Hughes and Mayor William Donald Schaefer were present representing the citizenry of Maryland and Baltimore. Present also were several hundred handpicked guests whose life's work and philanthropy on behalf of Israel had earned them a place in this company.

The VIPs were enjoying salmon baked in Russian pastry, called *kulebiaka*, and sliced-to-order eye-of-the-rib beef. From steaming chafing dishes on rolling carts, waiters served up broccoli flowers and Belgian carrots. Then the wine: Carmel Sauvignon blanc with the fish; Cabernet Sauvignon with the beef. After the entrée, green salad—in the European order of service. Then, for dessert: fresh strawberries and pineapple chunks in champagne glasses, with miniature strudel and brownies.

Extravagant as were the food and the service, the affair appeared to be just one more elegant dinner at the level of State Department hospitality. And it was, with one difference: This dinner was kosher.

At this time and place, that could only mean the caterer was Bluefeld—the menu, the food, the service, the style. For almost half a century Bluefeld dominated Baltimore's kosher catering business as no other kosher catering business has done before or since. The Bluefeld share of the market, according to Lou Bluefeld, now retired in Florida, was easily 70 percent.

The Bluefeld story began in 1937 with Bluefeld's (actually, Mrs. Bluefeld's) first catering job, in the old Workmen's Circle Hall on East Baltimore Street. "It was a wedding," Lou Bluefeld recalls. "My mother charged a dollar and a quarter a person." Mrs. Bluefeld had been running a concession stand at the Progressive Shore on the Magothy River (the shore facility was a part of the Brith Sholom Lodge). Success in that small community led to an established business operation in the Bluefeld home, first, beginning in 1937, at 3522 Greenspring Avenue; then, in 1940, at 3506 Auchentoroly Terrace. "Rabbi Drazin was our mentor. Our family belonged to his shul, Shaarei Tfiloh, so it was quite a natural relationship," Lou Bluefeld adds.

The story ended when the Bluefelds sold their business to Danielle Mosse, the daughter and granddaughter of Orthodox rabbis, and her husband, Georges, in March 1984. The business closed in the winter of 1998. "Since the Bluefelds were in business here," says Leonard "Lenny" Kaplan, who has been in the catering business for around forty years, "the kosher catering business in Baltimore has changed. Nobody holds the dominant position within it that Bluefeld once did. It is not likely that it will happen again. These days there are simply too many players."

Most in the Jewish community will not remember Bluefeld so much for the firm's presence in the higher reaches of State Department entertaining as for its catering of thousands of family Bar and Bat Mitzvahs, sweet sixteen parties, brotherhood and sisterhood donor dinners, synagogue and organizational dinners, annual dinners, birthday dinners, family circle parties, class reunions, and weddings—all over a period of some fifty years. Many in the Jewish community have spent a measurable part of their lives spearing hors d'oeuvres off passing trays at the Blue Crest banquet facilities at 401 Reisterstown Road.

There were other kosher caterers—Baida, Schleider, any number of Mom and Pop operations—but Bluefeld seemed to be different. The Bluefelds (Lou, Phil, Milton, and into the third generation, Brian, and Richard) were affable joiners. They were caterers, but they were marketing and public relations executives, too. "We were born and raised in Baltimore," Lou Bluefeld said. He continues:

We knew a lot of people, and we were creative and flexible.

We were the first kosher caterers to build fruit displays, substituting fruit for the much heavier desserts associated with kosher caterers. We were doing as many as fifteen and twenty affairs a week.

Our big break came in 1947. We were asked by Mrs. Joseph Meyerhoff to cater a reception for the Meyerhoff's son, Harvey, and his new bride, Lyn, at the Woodholme. The couple had been recently married in Chicago at the bride's family home, and Mrs. Meyerhoff wanted an affair that would be tasteful. Mrs. Meyerhoff, Rebecca, kept kosher, and so she wanted only a kosher affair—and the best. She called us.

But Mrs. Meyerhoff's choice of day of the week for the party surprised us—Monday. She chose Monday because she wanted it at the Woodholme Country Club and the club was closed on Monday. That meant she could have the whole place for her party. Of course, the Woodholme was not equipped to do kosher catering, so we had to bring everything in—dishes, equipment, the works.

The party was beautiful, Mrs. Meyerhoff was delighted. Word got around and the success of the affair and the family name launched us into a significant middle week business. We expanded our weekday business from there on out.

Bluefeld's catering of major affairs honoring dignitaries is legendary. Lou Bluefeld says, "It was an ego trip, no question about it. I enjoyed the recognition." The firm catered a party in the United Nations building in New York for 350 members of Hadassah and another for 7,000 people at an Israel Bond rally in the Washington Armory. When Israel's Prime Minister Menachem Begin visited the United States in 1980, Bluefeld got the call. "We sent our food and our cooks to the White House for a state dinner, and managed the meals at Blair House during the rest of Mr. Begin's stay." Bluefeld also did three parties for the Israeli Ambassador Mrs. Ahrens.

Mr. Bluefeld again recalls:

The way the process worked was interesting, We would prepare everything in Baltimore in our own kosher kitchen, and put it all in a truck. The doors were sealed, locked, and the loading of the food and the sealing of it in the truck were all overseen by both the FBI and our own *mashgiach*. When we got to Washington, the process was reversed.

The doors were unsealed and the food was unloaded and taken into the White House, or Blair House, wherever the party might have been, all under the watchful eye of our *mashgiach* and the FBI.

The Bluefelds sold the business to A.R.A. Services in 1969. They continued to manage it for seven years and bought it back in 1976; then in 1984 they sold it to Danielle and Georges Mosse.

In fifty years of catering the most lavish affairs, including those of the rich and the famous and the powerful from the world over, and creating sophisticated recipes that became a Bluefeld trademark after fifty years of serving every conceivable kosher dish—what Bluefeld item had proved the most popular?

"Our meat knish," Lou Bluefeld answers. "My mother's old recipe."

Shaarei Tfiloh: Center of a Neighborhood with No Name

It was the hub of a thickly populated area and ever-developing Jewish community.

It is easy to name a Jewish neighborhood that owed its very being to a particular synagogue. Beth Tfiloh was such an institution in its day; Chizuk Amuno on Eutaw Place (the present Beth Am) can be said to be another; include, too, Shaarei Zion at Park Heights and Hilldale. To this list one can surely add the neighborhood with no official name, an area only vaguely defined geographically: the streets leading to and from the Shaarei Tfiloh synagogue at Holmes Avenue and Liberty Heights Avenue, taking in Bryant, Whittier, and Orem Avenues, as well as Tioga Parkway and Auchentoroly Terrace.

"It was a neighborhood between neighborhoods," is the way Sylvia Bliss Mandy describes the several blocks centered around Liberty Heights Avenue, Gwynns Falls Parkway, and Reisterstown Road. "It's hard to know where the neighborhood ended but most everyone who lived there can tell you where it began—at the Shaarei Tfiloh synagogue at Liberty Heights and Holmes Avenue. If I had to give a name to the neighborhood I would call it the 'Shaarei Tfiloh neighborhood.'"

Some of the young people in the neighborhood went to elementary school at P.S. 64 in Forest Park; most went to P.S. 60 on Francis Street near Fulton Avenue; junior high for most was Garrison. The boys went to Forest Park or City, the girls to Forest Park or Western. "But most all went to Shaarei Tfiloh Hebrew School," Mrs. Mandy noted. "None of us can forget our teacher, a Mr. Gunner."

The neighborhood shopping center took in the 2400 block of Reisterstown Road between Bryant Avenue and Gwynns Falls Parkway: Sachs Brothers Pharmacy was at 2423; Dogoloff's grocery at 2429; Pear's deli at 2431; Silber's bakery at 2435. Wagner and Wagner opened in 1927 and served the neighborhood for almost half a century, into the mid-1970s. It was owned by Emanuel Wagner; Sidney Weinberg was a popular pharmacist who worked there. Charles "Charley" Wagner, nephew of Emanuel, worked there as delivery boy from the day he got his driver's license until he left for the military. Charley remembers: "We served customers as far south as Fulton Avenue, as far east as Auchentoroly Terrace, west to where Douglass High School, formerly Western High, is today, and north all the way to Liberty Heights and Burleith Avenue. Wagner and Wagner was a no-nonsense pharmacy. Hangin' out was at Sachs's down the street."

Pear's opened in 1930. Marian Pear Koenigsburg remembers: "It was a small deli, maybe four or five tables, but thanks to my mother's passion about good food we had a reputation far beyond our size. The Hecht department store family used to send their chauffeur in to buy sandwiches. My brother and I worked right alongside of my mother and father. We had no cooks or waitresses—we were it!" Pear's became Paul's when the Pear family sold the business in 1940. Meanwhile, Sylvan Dogoloff recalls that his father and mother opened their grocery store in the early 1930s. "My twin brother Mark and I worked here with my mother and father, David and Rose. It was your typical Jewish neighborhood grocery. Except we started out as a dairy store, converted it to a grocery store and then added a small deli."

Jews began moving into the community in the early 1920s, as part of the migration out north and west from the East Baltimore neighborhoods. The attraction at the beginning was not the synagogue but Druid Hill Park. "The park was everybody's backyard, an extension of the neighborhood," Mrs. Mandy says. "Before we went off to school we would go over to the tennis court office and get a permit good for times after we came home from school. Then when we came home, all we had to do was grab our racquets and head for our very own tennis courts. And we always checked into the Conservatory to see what kind of flower show may have been going on." Others from the neighborhood talked of horseback riding through the park (Hechter's Riding Academy was at McCulloh Street and Cloverdale Road, only a few blocks away) and bicycling: you rode your own bicycle or you could rent one from Davis's, up at Park Circle.

Mrs. Mandy has her own personal recollection of the High Holy Days in the neighborhood: "The streets bordering the shul were closed to traffic. The joy, the spirituality, seemed to me to vibrate through the sidewalks as young people in the neighborhood—Margery Schwartzman, Esther Cordish. Alan Behrend, Zelda Needle, Philip Needle, and I—walked to and from nearby Chizuk Amuno and Shaarei Zion. I lived at 1723 Gwynns Falls from the time I was two years old until I was married. My Dad helped found Shaarei Tfiloh and he supported it until his death in 1974."

Shaarei Tfiloh was founded and held its first services in 1920 at nearby 2218 Bryant Avenue. The new building facing Druid Hill Park was officially dedicated September 25, 1921. Among the founders were Louis Cordish, Solom Seidman, Harry Klaff, Alex Pleet, and Harry Lipsitz. Rabbi Nathan Drazin was rabbi from 1933 to 1964. Alumni remember cantors Abraham Selsky and Jacob Wahrman. An advertisement in the *Jewish Times* in 1921 announced the synagogue's opening sale of seats: "Men's seats, $5 and $10 and $15. Ladies seats, $5 and $10." And it offered this incentive: "The synagogue is ideally located, surrounded by the beautiful Druid Hill Park, and the structure is so designed to make it the coolest and most comfortable place to worship in Baltimore."

A story in the *Jewish Times* of September 23, 1923, reported:

> The cornerstone of the new synagogue was laid on July 10, 1921, and since then every effort was made to complete the structure for the High Holy Days, which begin on the eve of October 2.
>
> Prominent speakers will attend the dedication exercises proper on Sunday at 2:00 P.M. At Saturday morning's service, which is the first Sabbath service to be held in the new synagogue, Dr. Schaffer will deliver the first sermon. The synagogue has elected its new cantor who will officiate for the first service on Saturday morning.

Commenting on the synagogue as the center of the neighborhood, a later article (March 19, 1926) looked back and reflected on Shaarei Tfiloh: "The Shaarei Tfiloh synagogue, located at the intersection of Auchentoroly Terrace and Holmes Avenue, the hub of a thickly-populated and ever-developing Jewish community, has the unique distinction of being bordered on two sides by a natural park and having an unobstructed street frontage on three of its four sides. The completed edifice standing thus upon a completed location of unequalled prominence"—and here the writer may have gotten somewhat carried away—"an ideal spot, will in reality be a veritable Temple in history."

Edgar Silver lived at 2315 Orem Avenue, "two doors from Nathan Askin, a really great tennis player." He continues,

But my second home was Sachs's, owned by Ray and Milo Sachs. In that neighborhood, tennis was on everybody's mind because the clay courts of Druid Hill Park were ours to use—they helped make the park our own country club. On any day after school and most all day Saturday thirty or forty kids would gather at Sachs's. We talked tennis, we read about tennis, we played tennis, we replayed tennis—player by player, game by game. I remember Leonard Rodman, Sidney Kemper, Stanley Bond, Joe Leiter. But hanging out was for guys—it was a male, street corner fraternity. Girls were not included.

Years later when I ran and won in my first election for House of Delegates I felt that it was the gang at Sachs's from my boyhood days that put me in office. That neighborhood was where I got started in politics, listening to Leon Abramson, Maxwell Alpert, Jacob Edelman.

Gwynns Falls Parkway, Liberty Heights Avenue, Holmes Avenue and Auchentoroly Terrace, Sachs's and Wagner and Wagner, Dogoloff's, Pear's, the High Holy Days walks to Shaarei Tfiloh, and the clay tennis courts in the park—the neighborhood seemed to have everything but a name.

Reisterstown Road and Rogers Avenue: The Diner, Mandell-Ballow, the Crest

A generation has put the crossroads into the mythology of Jewish Baltimore.

Northwest Baltimore over the years has had any number of neighborhood centers that were popular with the Jewish community (Park Heights and Belvedere, Liberty Road and Old Court), and though vanished, they all remain memorable. One that bids fair to be among the most fondly remembered is the complex of stores, restaurants, movie theater, and synagogue close to and hugging the four corners of Reisterstown Road and Rogers Avenue. From 1956 well into the 1980s, this busy center offered visitors the well-known Baltimore family stores, the Crest movie theater, and Mandell-Ballow's delicatessen, all in the Hilltop Shopping Center. The Rogers Avenue Synagogue, a few blocks to the east, served congregants living in the neighborhood, including many who had moved to the Rogers Avenue community from West Baltimore. In the same area were Weiner's pharmacy, B&B food market, Greenfeld Brothers hardware, and Barry Levinson's legendary "Diner." For almost forty years, the area was a destination for a generation that would etch it into the continuing memory of Northwest Baltimore.

The Crest theater opened on February 26, 1949, with *Adventures of Don*

Juan, starring Errol Flynn and Viveca Lindfors. In those days, ticket prices were twenty-five cents for matinees Monday through Friday and forty cents in the evening and all day Saturday, Sundays, and holidays. Children were admitted for eighteen cents—all shows.

A full-page ad in the *Evening Sun* on February 25 announced the Crest's grand opening the next day and presented the theater as state of the art: "Seventeen hundred seats, air-conditioned, twin-smoking loges." There is no record of the paid admissions on opening day, but there didn't seem to be much competition around; downtown, the Century was showing the forgettable *Command Decision* with Clark Gable; upstairs at the Valencia wasn't much better—*History Is Made at Night* with Charles Boyer.

Mandell-Ballow was a Jewish deli in the "overwhelm them" style of both Mandell's of Baltimore Street and Ballow's of West North Avenue, offering monstrous sandwiches and desserts. The restaurant accommodated 300 at a time and during some of its years was open twenty-four hours; so it became a headquarters of sorts for politicians choosing their candidates, for businessmen striking their deals, and race track types touting their favorites. There was a banquet hall downstairs, the Fiesta Room, which was the scene of many a Bar and Bat Mitzvah party.

Jay Mandell, son of proprietor Joseph Mandell, worked at Mandell-Ballow after he graduated college, in 1963. He recalls, "We were doing business in a time before the fast food chains opened, and so were really 'the' place to eat in Northwest Baltimore. When the show broke at the Crest hundreds of people flooded our doors. They formed a line all the way back to the Crest. We had a soda fountain with stools and our own bakery. Our big seller was our Number Three sandwich—corned beef, coleslaw, and Russian dressing.

"Busy? We had three shifts working, maybe a hundred people, just to keep the place going."

Jay's sister, Barbara Mandell Desser, looks back:

I was in high school in 1958 and worked after school and weekends in the deli, wherever they needed me. At the register, in the bake shop, at the soda fountain. I helped make sundaes. Do you know that we had green, pink, blue, and yellow whipped cream?

But our pastries were something very special. We had a German baker named Ludwig, and, with my father's encouragement, he used only natural ingredients, no synthetics. He baked mouthwatering eclairs, Danish, cream pies and Napoleons.

But everything served at Mandell-Ballow was special. We pickled our own corned beef. Nothing you buy in a deli today compares with the quality we served at Mandell-Ballow at the Hilltop Shopping Center.

The restaurant was destroyed by fire in the mid-1960s and never reopened.

Also in the center were Saler's dairy, Sheer and Dreibon kosher butchers, Eddie's supermarket, Barcelona nut and candy, Hilltop bowling alley. And Holzman's bakery.

Holzman's was one of the most popular of the Jewish-owned retail bakeries in Baltimore. At one time, according to Willie Holzman, there were as many as six Holzman's bakeries in operation throughout the area. Mr. Holzman remembers his bakery in the Hilltop Shopping Center: "We opened in 1948 and we were there until 1979—thirty one years. Hilltop in those days was a very busy shopping center, and ours was a busy store. It took twelve people to keep it operating."

Across Reisterstown Road from Hilltop was the Diner, gone these many years and now occupied by Hilltop Liquors. "The Diner," according to Irving Lansman, whose A&L kosher food distribution company was a supplier to the Diner, "was founded right after the war by Mike Siegel, who sold it to the Stamas brothers. The menu was very Jewish—they featured bagels and lox, blintzes, Matzoh ball soup, and, at their counter, Halavah."

As it has been so engagingly portrayed in the movie of the same name, the Diner was more than a restaurant; it was a hangout for a group of young neighborhood men going through the teenage rites of passage, using wit and verbal sparring to ease the way.

On the High Holy Days, Rogers Avenue at Reisterstown Road became a scene of milling crowds coming and going to the nearby Rogers Avenue Synagogue. The synagogue had its roots deep in the West Baltimore of the early twentieth century, and in 1929 it emerged in Baltimore history as the Ohr Knesseth Israel congregation. In 1950, the Anshe Sphard congregation of 4 North Broadway and the Ohr Knesseth Israel Congregation of West Franklin Street merged to form the Ohr Knesseth Israel-Anshe Shphard, known, beginning in 1951, as the Rogers Avenue synagogue, at 3910 West Rogers Avenue. (In 1993 the Rogers Avenue synagogue merged with Beth Jacob.)

IN THE LATE 1970S AND EARLY 1980S the Reisterstown and Rogers area was caught in the harsh socioeconomic changes of those years: In time, the movie house, the Diner, the synagogue, Weiner's pharmacy, B&B food market, Greenfeld's hardware, and many of the stores in the center either closed or left the Rogers Avenue and Reisterstown Road area and opened elsewhere. The center itself, built by the Myerberg Brothers and designed by architect Julius Myerberg, was sold to Steven Sibel.

The buildings that housed the familiar and wildly popular Jewish institutions once crowding the Reisterstown Road and Rogers Avenue area are all still there, and they remain recognizable, too. But for Jews who have vivid memories of Mandell-Ballow, the Crest, Weiner's, the Rogers Avenue Synagogue, and the rest, these building are monuments to another era.

Menus from Nates and Leon's deli, ca. 1940. From 1937, when Nates Herr and Leon Shaivitz opened shop at North and Linden Avenues, until 1967, when it closed, Nates and Leon's may have been Baltimore's most popular deli. It owed its spectacular success to its hours (open twenty four hours a day) and, according to Nates Herr himself, the food: "Our Number Three sandwich—corned beef, Russian dressing, and coleslaw. Could never be beat." Their sandwiches were monstrous and available in dizzying combinations; their desserts of strawberry shortcake, Napoleons, and eclairs were little short of intimidating.

Take Your Troubles Out of the Kitchen
---Eat Regularly at Nates & Leons

Plan your meals so the family can eat here at least once a week. You and the cook will enjoy the holiday and everybody will enjoy the food. You just can't help it. Everything at Nates & Leons tastes like more . . . and costs less than if you prepared it yourself.

PLATTERS

"Justly Famous"
Please Order By Number:

No. 51—Franks and Potato Salad		.50
No. 52—Franks and Baked Beans		.50
No. 125—Smoked King Fish, Hard Boiled Egg, Slaw, Lettuce and Tomato		1.00
No. 126—Genuine Portugese Skinless and Boneless Sardines, Slaw, Hard Bpiled Egg, Lettuce and Tomato		1.25
No. 127—Cold Baked Virginia Ham, Potato Salad, Hard Boiled Egg, Lettuce and Tomato		1.25
No. 128—Corned Beef and Egg Platter, Salad, Lettuce and Tomato		.75
No. 129—Salami and Egg Platter, Salad, Lettuce and Tomato		.75
No. 130—Bologna and Egg Platter, Salad, Lettuce and Tomato		.75
No. 131—Tongue and Egg Platter, Salad, Lettuce and Tomato		.75
No. 132—Order of Bacon and Eggs		.40

SOUPS

Fresh Soup .20   Canned Soup .25

EGGS AND OMELETS

Two Eggs, any style .25

FOOD AT   ITS BEST

Boltansky's grocery store, northwest corner
of Lombard Street and Central Avenue, ca.
1943. George Boltansky stands on the left;
his twelve-year-old daughter, Shirley, joins
him behind the counter. Boltansky had been
in the moving business, but when an opportunity to buy the grocery appeared, he
seized it—for thirteen dollars. The store
sold coddies, loose cigarettes, work gloves,
bags of coal, bundles of wood, corn-cob
pipes, and Tootsie Pops, along with meats
and groceries. The meat showcase to the
left was meter operated; it required seventy-five cents each night to keep the case
refrigerated through the night until morning.
Boltansky sold out in 1944.

The Sisterhood of Har Sinai goes to war. From 1941 through to the end of World War II, Har Sinai women operated a canteen and hostelry in the vestry room of the synagogue. The ladies provided Saturday-night sleeping accommodations for about twenty servicemen and served them a giant Sunday morning breakfast. *Left to right:* Wilhelmina (Mrs. Martin) Dannenberg; Rosemund (Mrs. Irvin) Kaufman; Jeanette (Mrs. Bernard) Klein; Connie (Mrs. Milton) Levinson; Oetz (Mrs. Meyer) Lebow; Olga (Mrs. Louis) Ashman; and, seated, Mollie (Mrs. Joseph) Wase.

Har Sinai Sisterhood president Nora (Mrs. Jay) Holly poses with several servicemen at one of its justly famous Sunday-morning hospitality breakfasts.

The rabbi, Captain Manuel Poliakoff (*center*), and cantor, Corporal Martin Willen (*right*), both of Baltimore and the 115th Infantry Regiment, 29th Division, conduct Rosh Hashanah services in Rheydt Castle, Munchen-Gladbach, Germany, in the fall of 1944. Private first class Abraham Mirmelstein of Newport News, Virginia, holds the Torah. The national wire services picked up this remarkable story. These were believed to be the first Jewish services held as far east as the Rhein River by Allied troops. Even more remarkable, the castle once had belonged to one of Hitler's most notorious henchmen, Paul Joseph Goebbels.

Shaarei Zion congregational dinner,
February 28, 1945.

Left, facing page: The Trenton Democratic Club Softball Team, with spectators at a respectful distance, poses for the camera in about 1946. The club was headquarters to James H. "Jack" Pollack, political boss and kingmaker of the Fourth District; the team's tee shirts thus advertised the James Pollack Insurance Company. "Dutch" Baer, back row, second from left, continued to play a coach's role in men's softball.

Left: In 1947 the S.S. *President Warfield*, clandestinely converted in Baltimore from Chesapeake Bay steamer to passenger-carrying transport, embarked for service to the Haganah, carrying Jewish refugees out of Europe to Palestine. On her maiden voyage, as she neared Tel Aviv late at night, fully loaded with refugees who had boarded in Sète, France, British destroyers pulled up alongside, flooded the ship with light, and ordered it into Haifa. The refugees held up a huge plank displaying the name "President Warfield" and then defiantly flipped it over to show the reverse, which read, "Haganah Ship *Exodus*, 1947." Passengers were ordered to reboard ships for return to France. They refused and the ship was ordered to Germany. (Courtesy of the Chesapeake Maritime Museum.)

Many synagogues sponsored scout troops, but in 1947 the Jewish Educational Alliance received a charter for Troop 102 in East Baltimore. The troop's founding committee consisted of Joseph Cushner, George J. Friedman, and Robert I. Michaelson; Scoutmaster was Herbert R. Goldstein. The Alliance closed in 1951, merging with the Jewish Community Center on Park Heights Avenue.

CHARTERED BY CONGRESS — JUNE 15, 1916

BOY SCOUTS OF AMERICA

BE PREPARED

TROOP CHARTER

GRANTED TO

THE JEWISH EDUCATIONAL ALLIANCE

upon its proper application through its duly authorized representative to carry on the Boy Scout Program for

CHARACTER BUILDING : CITIZENSHIP TRAINING

subject to the provisions of the Constitution and By-Laws and rules and regulations of the National Council of the Boy Scouts of America for one year.

BOY SCOUT TROOP

#102, BALTIMORE, MD.

TROOP COMMITTEE

JOSEPH CUSHNER, CHM'N. & INST. REP.   GEORGE J. FRIEDMAN
ROBERT L. MICHAELSON

SCOUTMASTER

ROBERT R. GOLDSTEIN

ASSISTANT SCOUTMASTERS

These officials have been duly certified and are officially registered by the National Council to meet the responsibilities of their respective offices in accordance with the provisions of the Constitution and By-Laws of the Boy Scouts of America.

IN TESTIMONY WHEREOF the National Council has caused this charter to be signed by its officers and its corporate seal to be affixed.

DATED DECEMBER 31, 1947
220

HONORARY PRESIDENT   HONORARY VICE-PRESIDENT

HONORARY VICE-PRESIDENT   PRESIDENT

CHIEF SCOUT   CHIEF SCOUT EXECUTIVE

Forest Park High School, ca. 1950. Many Jewish young people who lived in Forest Park started their public school education by going, first, to elementary school at P.S. 64 at Maine Avenue and Garrison Boulevard, then to Garrison Junior High School at Garrison Boulevard and Barrington Road, and then to Forest Park High at Eldorado Avenue and Chatham Road.

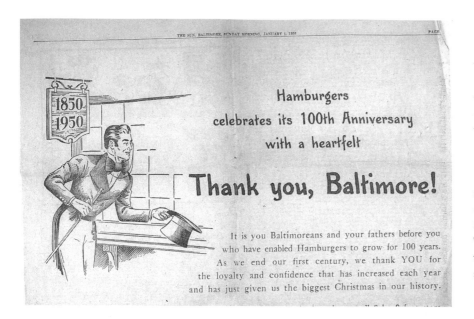

1850
1950

Hamburgers
celebrates its 100th Anniversary
with a heartfelt

Thank you, Baltimore!

It is you Baltimoreans and your fathers before you
who have enabled Hamburgers to grow for 100 years.
As we end our first century, we thank YOU for
the loyalty and confidence that has increased each year
and has just given us the biggest Christmas in our history.

The elegantly dressed dandy who appeared in many of Isaac Hamburger and Sons advertisements and had become familiar to generations of Baltimoreans announced the firm's centennial in January 1950.

Below: At an event held at the Southern Hotel, employees staged a skit spoofing management. *From the left:* Herb Rudolph in coonskin hat, Rae Rady Simmerman, Harry Shocket, Herb Weyrich, Felix Schreiber, and Walter Abramson. The patriarch— his portrait hanging from the window—seems to smile knowingly.

Purim festival at Shaarei Zion, 1956. This synagogue—having located in Lower Park Heights Avenue (at 3459) in the early 1920s—was one of two synagogues that led the movement of Baltimore's Jewish population north and west along the Park Heights Avenue corridor. At about the same time, the Shearith Israel synagogue, founded by German Jews and located at 2105 McCulloh Street, opened its "suburban branch" at the southeast corner of Park Heights and Glen Avenues—in Upper Park Heights.

The original Pimlico Hotel opened in 1823 at what became 5301 Park Heights Avenue and catered to Pimlico's racing crowd. In 1952 Leon Shaivitz and Nates Herr of the famous Nates and Leon's deli took over the hotel and converted it into a first-class, white-tablecloth restaurant. The Pimlico Hotel offered a fourteen-page menu, with more than 100 entrees, a complete Chinese menu, a full page of "suggestions" that changed daily, and hot, steamed crabs— and on weekends the soft lights, music, nightclub atmosphere, and dancing in the popular Cavalier Lounge. The Pimlico Hotel on Park Heights Avenue closed in 1982.

The legendary Rabbi Samuel Rosenblatt in 1955. He served Beth Tfiloh from 1927 until he retired in 1972. Born in Bratislava, which is now the capital of the Slovak Republic, he came to the United States at age ten. His long list of academic achievements included election to Phi Beta Kappa at City College of New York, studies at the Jewish Theological Seminary in New York, a doctorate from Columbia University, and post-graduate studies in Palestine. Rabbi Rosenblatt spoke nine languages, wrote ten books, and taught at Johns Hopkins University. Many Jewish families moved to Forest Park to be in his congregation. He died in 1983.

Purim at Shaarei Tfiloh in the mid-1950s.
People sometimes referred to the synagogue—founded in 1923— as the "shul in
the park" because it overlooks Druid Hill
Park at Auchentoroly Terrace and Liberty
Heights Avenue. It once commanded strong
loyalty from the Reisterstown Road, Liberty
Heights, Gwynns Falls Parkway, and Mondawmin neighborhoods. Shaarei Tfiloh remains a functioning synagogue.

Above: Arts and crafts at Camp Milldale on Mt. Gilead Road, August 1959. Camp Milldale was one of eight summer camps that the Jewish Community Center operated in Park Heights and Owings Mills. The camps offered programming from kindergarten through eighth grade.

Right: A young puppeteer helps stage a Chanukah show at the Jewish Community Center at 5700 Park Heights Avenue in December 1972. The Jewish Community Center assumed the role that originally the Jewish Educational Alliance and the YM and YWHA played in the community. This Park Heights, or "in-town," JCC now serves mostly the populations of Orthodox Jews and newly arrived Russian Jews living in the area. In 1978 a new and much larger community center opened in Owings Mills.

Epilogue

Owings Mills and Beyond, Still Moving
North and West

*How far north and west will the
Jewish community move?*

Communities come into being when and where a critical mass of people choose to live, for whatever reason. Communal institutions sometimes materialize in anticipation of people's arrival, and sometimes they follow or catch up to them. This rhythm—leading and catching up—characterizes the history of the development of Baltimore's Jewish communities. East Baltimore in the mid-nineteenth century set the pattern. German Jews coming to America in the 1830s were drawn to those streets where the commerce already was. Being of the trading class themselves, they saw opportunity to live and work among established merchants and so make their way in the new world. In the 1880s, when the Russian Jews arrived in great numbers, East Baltimore was already a well-established Jewish community, with institutions functioning to serve both the Jews of the existing community and the newcomers. Predictably, the new arrivals were quick to find and settle into East Baltimore.

The next Jewish community, Eutaw Place, came into being when the German Jewish merchants living and working in East Baltimore perceived, first, that their hard-earned status as "Americans" was being threatened by the arrival in East Baltimore of the Russian Jews—their Orthodoxy, their "old country" dress, manner, and speech; and second, that they were ready for a lifestyle of affluence.

When these German Jews moved to Eutaw Place, they found themselves entering an established and prestigious non-Jewish neighborhood. But in a very few years, the German Jewish families of Eutaw Place, though remaining very much a part of Baltimore's larger Jewish community, created their own institutions to serve their own needs and way of life.

The Russian Jews of East Baltimore, too, were becoming more "Ameri-

The Jewish Museum of Maryland consists of two historic synagogues and a modern museum building. The Lloyd Street Synagogue, on the northeast corner of Lloyd and Watson Streets, was built in 1845 and is among the oldest synagogue buildings in America, and the first to be erected in Maryland. Directly across Watson Street is the museum building itself. Next to it is B'nai Israel Synagogue, which was founded in 1873. The congregation moved into this building, formerly occupied by the Chizuk Amuno Congregation, in 1895. In the year 2000 the Jewish Museum of Maryland celebrates the fortieth anniversary of its founding.

can," and they also sought the class implications of "suburban" living and a life that was not lived "over the store." They leapfrogged over Eutaw Place to Park Heights Avenue.

They had good reason to do so. Some Jewish families had already established themselves in and among the Park Heights Avenue Jewish middle class. In the early 1920s Shaarei Zion formed in Lower Park Heights in anticipation of Orthodox families moving in; Shearith Israel opened a "suburban" branch uptown at Park Heights and Glen Avenue to serve their mostly German Jewish congregants already living in the area and those who, it was clear, would be very soon. With the two synagogues functioning on Park Heights Avenue beginning in the 1920s and early 1930s, the flood gates opened; and in a matter of a few years the entire Park Heights corridor, from Park Circle to the city line at Slade Avenue, became a Jewish neighborhood. The Jewish Community Center, kosher butchers, synagogues, Hebrew schools, the Baltimore Hebrew University, and agencies of the Associated Jewish Charities followed closely behind the populace.

Following World War II, the suburbs beckoned—houses with spacious lawns, good schools, and the tone of upscale suburban life itself attracted the Jews of Park Heights and Forest Park, who moved just a little further north and west, over the city line into Stevenson and its environs, and even further west into the Liberty Road corridor. As was expected, synagogues, schools, and merchants catering to the Jewish trade followed.

All the while that Jews were moving into the Park Heights, Pikesville-Stevenson-Liberty Road areas, a little-noticed phenomenon was occurring in Jewish demographics. Baltimore's Jews were on the move again. It was again north and west into what was once another traditionally non-Jewish stronghold, Owings Mills. Watching this latest movement into Owings Mills was Robert Hiller, then executive vice president of the Associated Jewish Charities. He recalled:

> It was clear that the center of the Jewish community was shifting. We wanted to know where it was going, and when it would settle down.
>
> Working closely with my associate Carmi Schwartz and some knowledgeable builders and land developers who were members of the Associated, we became aware that a huge shopping center was going to be built in Owings Mills—right in the northwest corridor. That could only mean new families moving in, and new homes, schools, and institutions. We studied the roads and the transportation systems. With the advice of good counsel, in 1970 we bought land in Owings Mills at Gwynnbrook and Walnut Avenues. We were encouraged by the data from a survey we had commissioned earlier in 1968, "Jewish Community of Metropolitan Baltimore; A Population Study."

What the Associated learned was that from 1968 to 1986 the population in the Pikesville—Owings Mills area had just about doubled. The trickle into this area beginning in the 1960s had, by the 1980s, become a small flood.

In this study, when asked what it was they were looking for when planning to move into a new neighborhood, the most frequent responses were "higher proportion of Jews" combined with "availability of Jewish facilities" (or what one would call "Jewish identity"). Transportation was a strong second. In this articulated lifestyle preference, Mr. Hiller could read the future, and it was Owings Mills.

As it would turn out, the Associated, armed with the facts from its survey, had called it right; in terms of numbers, Owings Mills was where the immediate future of the community lay. Not surprisingly, right on schedule with Mr. Hiller's vision, in 1978 the Jewish Community Center opened on its forty-acre site in Owings Mills—or, at least, the first of the buildings in the complex did, the Youth Services Building. "At the same time," Mr. Hiller said, "the Associated made a long-term commitment to its Jewish Community Center campus on Park Heights Avenue."

As has been the historical pattern, synagogues both anticipate and follow their congregants. By the time a second study came out in 1986, informing the community that of the 91,700 Jews living in the Baltimore area, 29,766 (about a third) were living in Pikesville–Owings Mills, the Jews of that expansive community were already worshipping in new synagogues or had plans to open synagogues, and this time as far out as Reisterstown.

Rabbi Aaron Gaber, spiritual leader of the thirteen-year-old Adat Chayim Synagogue at Cockeys Mill Road in Reisterstown, is thirty-one and says his personal profile mirrors the congregation's. "We are mostly young people, living and worshipping far removed from our parents' and grandparents' roots. In the case of our members born and raised in the Baltimore area, that means East Baltimore, or Lake Drive, or Forest Park or Park Heights. As history goes, we are new frontier Jews, starting a new chapter in Jewish Baltimore's history."

Rabbi Jay R. Goldstein of Beth Israel on Crondall Lane in Owings Mills observes of his congregation, "Beth Israel has an interesting mix of people—those who have been with the congregation when we were on Liberty Road, those who have recently moved to Owings Mills, and those in their sixties and seventies who still live in the Park Heights corridor.

"But here in Owings Mills, change is in the air. There are many signs that more Jewish families are moving out here and that institutions and commercial enterprises are responding to their wants and needs."

Temple Emanuel on Berryman's Lane in Reisterstown was started in 1955 to serve the then growing Jewish population of Liberty Road. "Our congregants," Rabbi Gustav Buchdahl says, "did not for the most part connect to Baltimore's traditional Jewish communities—Pikesville and Forest Park for example. They did not grow up in that tradition, with that history. They no longer feel that they share the same history, the same memories, the same sense of neighborhood. We out here are a new kind of Jewish community."

Rabbi Buchdahl cautions against calling Owings Mills or even Reisterstown the "furthest out" of Baltimore's Jewish communities. "It is hard to know at this point in time how many Jews are living, or will be living, in Carroll County. But we do know that Jews are moving out here in increasing numbers." The notion is supported by Rabbi Seymour Essrog, rabbi of the twenty-year-old Beth Shalom of Carroll County in Taylorsville, about ten miles south of Westminster. "Six years ago," he says, "we had twenty children in our religious school. Today we have seventy. Many of our congregants have moved out here from the north and west sections of Baltimore County. They have never been a part of Northwest Baltimore City or its tradition. They are building their own Jewish community and we simply cannot predict the strength or the size of it."

We do know this: the Owings Mills Jewish community now also includes the Kol Ami congregation; and, in the planning stages, main or Auxiliary facilities of Har Sinai, Beth Tfiloh, Bais Yaakov School for Girls, and the Etz Chayim Center for Jewish Studies. If someday the heart of Maryland's Jewish population were to be Carroll County, with Westminster at its center, that would put us just ten miles from Pennsylvania—a long way from East Baltimore and the 1830s, when and where it all began.

Generations have come and gone since the great migrations of Jews from Central and Eastern Europe found their way into Baltimore. They arrived with far-reaching dreams for a Jewish community in which they could take their place, but whatever the size of those dreams they are small indeed against the record of the years.

Owings Mills, Reisterstown, and Carroll County may be the frontier for Baltimore's Jewish community geographically, but in terms of accomplishment, of commitment to enriching the quality of life in Baltimore—in the arts, academia, business, and civic life—the frontier appears nowhere in sight. How it would have lightened the hearts of the Jewish immigrants arriving in Baltimore with their fears and wavering dreams if they could have known what kind of Baltimore Jewish community they would help bring into being and leave as a legacy to their children and their children's children.

Index

JEWISH BALTIMORE

by Gilbert Sandler

Designed by Kathleen Szawiola, set by the designer in Filosofia,
and printed by The Maple Press.

Library of Congress Cataloging-in-Publication Data

Sandler, Gilbert.

Jewish Baltimore : a family album / Gilbert Sandler.

    p.   cm.

Contains index.

ISBN 0-8018-6427-5

1. Jews—Maryland—Baltimore—History—19th century. 2. Jews—
Maryland—Baltimore—History—20th century. 3. Baltimore (Md.)—
Ethnic relations. I. Title.

F189.B19 S17   2000

975.2'6004924—dc21

99-050920